TEACHABLES II

HOMEMADE TOYS THAT TEACH

By Rhoda Redleaf

Illustrations by Ellen Krans

TOYS 'n THINGS PRESS
A Division of Resources for Child Caring, Inc.

© 1987 by Toys 'n Things Press
a division of
Resources for Child Caring, Inc.

All rights reserved.
Printed in the United States of America.

Published by Toys 'n Things Press
a division of
Resources for Child Caring, Inc.
906 North Dale Street
St. Paul, Minnesota 55103

Distributed by Gryphon House, Inc.
P. O. Box 275
Mt. Rainier, Maryland 20712

Library of Congress Catalog Number: 87-050215

ISBN: 0-934140-41-3

First Edition

1 2 3 4 5 6 7 8 9 10

The wealth of homemade ideas in this book
and its predecessor,
TEACHABLES FROM TRASHABLES,
is a tribute to the creativity
and energy of the wonderful child care
teachers, family day care providers,
trainers and others who make up the
Minnesota child care community.

TABLE OF CONTENTS

MISCELLANEOUS

INDEX

ACKNOWLEDGEMENTS

This book would not have been possible without the assistance of many people over a very long period of time. Since many of the ideas shared in this book came from curriculum idea fairs sponsored by Resources for Child Caring, past and present staff members are to be thanked for their indirect contribution to this book.

More directly however, I wish to thank those who contributed the toy ideas and activities to our original fairs. If they, in turn, had adapted the idea from a teacher, friend, or colleague, I express my apologies to the unknown, and therefore unacknowledged, originator.

Maxine McPherson
Linda Stoltenberg
Julie Nelson
June Smith
Kathy Reber
Donna Glaser
JoAnne Peterson
Ardis Kysar
Mary Nordby
Connie Koran
Audrey Robertson
Carol Brennan
Irene Trigonis
Betty Delmedica
Kathy Tope
Candace Nadler
Dianna Diers
Carol Adams
Zehra Ansari
Daphyn Nordeen

Lois Brokering
Joyce Poor
Lin D. Ann Burman
Valerie Lewicki
Marie Anthony
Starr Alson
Joanne Searles
Kathy Koczera
Cynthia Behling
Gayle Forman
Karen Boehne-Warner
Carla Weigel
Beth Overstad
Betty Klein
Frances Moore
Priscilla Williams
Mike Tittle
Doris Furlong
Sonja Irlbeck
Kim Reiner

I also want to thank those most closely involved in the production of this book. In my opinion, a better publishing staff than Toys 'n Things Press is not possible. Editor, Jill Hix; illustrator, Ellen Krans; and editorial staff, Ceil Meade and Martha Malan, are to be commended for their excellent work.

Finally, thank you to my family for their support and encouragement, and to my grandson, Nathaniel, who gave the toys the definitive Toddler Test.

INTRODUCTION

Welcome to **TEACHABLES II** -- a book designed to inspire your toy-making talents. Using readily available household items, you can create 77 different toys for your children from infants to school-agers. The toys are presented alphabetically in categories based on the main material used in construction. Each activity includes two descriptive sections ("How to Use It" and "What It Does"), a materials list, and step-by-step directions for making the toy. In some cases, we have offered alternate materials and variation games.

The **How to Use It** section describes activities and ways children of different ages might use the toys. Most of the toys described can be adapted for use by preschool or young school-age children. Our suggested uses are just a beginning. Since good toys are versatile and let the child do the creating, children will undoubtedly find their own uses and should be encourged to do so.

In addition, our age suggestions should not be taken as absolute. Remember that children grow and develop at their own individual pace and with varying interests, so the appeal of particular ideas and activities will vary for each child. We have indicated, however, toys that are appropriate for toddlers. You will find these listed in the Index at the back of the book.

The **What It Does** column describes what skills each activity teaches or helps develop. The toys and activities and the skills they encourage are also included in the Index. Many of these encourage development in more than one area, and therefore may be listed in the Index more than once.

Use this book in the way that works best for you. You might let the children select the first "project". Make it a group effort and get them involved, keeping safety considerations in mind. If your child needs extra practice in a certain skill area, such as visual perception, check the Index for suggestions on the most appropriate toys.

We hope you will find **TEACHABLES II** useful as a guide to creative toys. Don't stop here! Use your imagination and the techniques you've learned to create more toys. Let the children see that making toys can be as much fun as playing with them.

Enjoy!

WHY TEACHABLES: A LOOK AT LEARNING

Much has been written in recent years about the importance of learning in early childhood. Unfortunately, a trend to push for earlier and earlier "academic" learning has been the result. In reaction to this, the National Association for the Education of Young Children has adopted a strong position statement for developmentally appropriate practice in working with young children. This positon emphasizes the importance of play in fostering learning.

Young children learn through direct hands-on manipulation and a great deal of repetition. They learn best if they are at play and the learning emerges as a by-product of that play. By asking questions, helping to make associations between known and unknown, and stimulating interest and curiosity through toy selection and activities offered, adults enhance the learning environment. A constant flow of brand new toys is not needed. Often, reorganization or additions to familiar toys and activities will reawaken the child's interest.

The items described in this book are intended to be used in play, and in that sense they are toys. But they also provide stimulation for major developmental and learning processes. I like to think of them as toys which enable teaching through play, hence, "Teachables".

Most toys included in this book serve multiple purposes and can be used in many different ways. We have suggested a few and hope you and your children will discover many more. In addition, the use of many items can be expanded by exchanging or substituting activities among toys of similar type.

A few general suggestions may help you in maximizing some of the learning potential:

1. Understand that repetition is a necessary part of learning. Activities which quickly bore adults often continue to be of interest to children. Many of the toys and games may strike adults as versions of "the same old thing". To children, however, each one is a new experience, and it is the children's enjoyment that is the most important consideration.

2. You can vary the difficulty of matching games by making the discrimination tasks more complex or very simple.

3. Capitalize on the interests of your children. For instance, a child who has no interest in matching games, but who loves dinosaurs, will often participate willingly if the "matches" are of different types of dinosaurs. A

child's attention span grows directly in relation to his or her interest in the activity.

4. It is best to present one skill or task at a time. Many matching games in this book include multiple matching criteria. This is to make the game more versatile in the long run, but initially, you should emphasize one criteria (i. e., color). Generally, older age children will show interest in the more complicated multiple criteria tasks.

5. Recognize the "literacy" value of cue cards. These cards serve not only as "clues" to playing a game, but also introduce the concept of symbols representing meaning, a pre-reading skill.

6. Children's exposure to learning about games with rules is a slowly evolving process. Young children frequently agree to rules but have no idea how to follow them and are not at all interested in the process. It is best to avoid too many rules or "real games" that feature winners.

It is our hope that this book will help people who care for children understand and enjoy the learning potential inherent in play and to cherish the creativity and imaginative playfulness of childhood.

GENERAL CONSIDERATIONS IN TOY MAKING

HELPFUL HINTS FOR TOY MAKING

Once you have chosen a toy to make, look at the "What You Need to Make It" and "How to Make It" instructions before beginning. Note any safety considerations, particularly if materials will be used by toddlers. A substitute material can be used in toy construction if you prefer. Generally we have tried to use tools and materials that are readily available to everyone.

Here are some suggestions about selecting and using materials for toy making:

Glue

All-purpose white glues are usually marked "nontoxic" and, if so, are good for toymaking. Many other glues contain substances that could be harmful if swallowed, so be sure to check the glue you use. If the bottle is not marked "nontoxic", choose another brand.

Felt Tip Markers

Markers add color and are easy to use, but they do have limitations. "Permanent" markers are usually toxic and should be avoided. Waterbased markers are usually safe, but toys made with them should be covered with clear contact paper if there is any chance they might be chewed on or become wet. Instead of markers, use contact paper cut in shapes when making toddler toys.

Contact Paper

Using contact paper in construction allows for easy cleaning and may increase the life of the toy. Brightly colored contact paper also helps attract a child's attention to the toy. Usually found in variety or hardware stores, contact paper is a good investment for any serious toymaker. Here's how to use it:

1. Measure amount needed and lay flat on the table with covering side up.

2. Twist edges to loosen covering so it can be removed.

3. Carefully peel away cover and leave contact paper on table with the sticky side up.

14

4. Lay items to be covered face down on the contact. If needed, place a second piece of contact on top of game pieces, sticky side down.

5. Smooth by rubbing with fingers and cut pieces out. For single-side coverage, fold edges over the sides of the game piece or artwork.

Pattern contact papers can be used in the same way as wrapping paper.

Coding Dots

Coding dots come in all sizes and colors and are generally available in office supply stores. They usually come in boxes of 1,000 dots per color, so it is a good idea to find other people who would like to share materials. Some craft shops and teacher supply stores have mixed colors of dots or labels and some office supply stores will sell individual sheets or have smaller packages.

Wrapping Paper

Wrapping paper is very useful for making puzzles or many kinds of matching games. You can use new or "used" wrapping paper. Look for attractive papers with 6 to 8 or more picture items that are repeated. You can use paper with an overall scene such as a playground, forest, Sesame Street or Walt Disney scene, or papers designed with all different kinds of items such as trucks, rocket ships, animals, flowers, etc. repeated many times.

Plastic Containers, Lids

All sizes and shapes of containers and lids can be used in many ways in making and storing games. For ease in cutting plastic, heat scissors or knife over a flame. The heat melts the plastic and makes it easier to cut. Cutting this way also produces a smoother edge on the plastic that is safer and looks better. Cutting plastic this way should be done by adults. Flames and sharp knives are not safe for children to use.

Juice Can Lids

These lids work especially well in many toddler toys or matching games. Be sure to use only the smooth edge lids that come from the pull-tab containers (currently popular on frozen juices). Pictures can be glued to the lids or they can be used in play as anything from play money to "pancakes" to cook. Let the children invent uses.

Empty Rolls From Tape

Plastic or paper ones can be used in ring toss, as wheels, or in other imaginative ways.

Stickers and Seals

Children love stickers and will be happy just to stick them in books, but adults can convert them into matching or board games. Books of stickers from flowers to dinosaurs can be found in teacher supply stores, instrumental and sheet music stores, and dime stores. Party shops and drug stores also have stickers, but they are more expensive and you have to be sure the packages contain more than one sheet of each sticker. Interesting games can be made using assorted holiday stickers. Look for at least six different versions of the same category (i.e.: 6 pumpkins, 6 butterflies, etc.)

SAFETY CONSIDERATIONS IN MAKING AND USING TOYS

Always consider the safety needs of children when you make toys. Safe toys for children meet these tests:

THEY ARE CLEAN

Wash all materials and containers thoroughly before using.

THEY HAVE NO SHARP EDGES

Tape or round off corners. Take special care in removing lids from coffee cans to be sure they are smooth along the rim. Sand and oil all materials that might splinter.

THEY ARE TOO BIG TO SWALLOW

A general rule is that an object should be approximately 1" x 1 1/2" in size. If you must use small objects, tie a few of them together to make them bigger. When using sponges in toddler projects, be sure to make the pieces even larger so they can't be swallowed and are less likely to be chewed. Do not use staples in toys being made for infants or toddlers. Sew or tape together toys such as the Easy Flannel Board, Furry Animal Friend, etc., if they will be handled by toddlers.

THEY ARE MADE OF NONTOXIC MATERIALS

Do not use any material that could be harmful if eaten, chewed or smelled! Read package instructions to make sure that markers and glue or other adhesives are nontoxic and safe for use with children. Do not use styrofoam pellets or packing materials in toys to be used by toddlers. Toys using styrofoam are not generally intended for use by toddlers. The same toys could be made from wood, cardboard, or plastic. The styrofoam could also be covered with clear contact to make it more "bite" resistant.

NOTE: Although the instructions for toys in this book have been written with "kid-proofed" tests in mind, no one can guarantee the absolute safety of these toys or procedures. We urge parents and teachers to use care and common sense to make all toys as safe as possible. Most of these toys are intended to be made by adults for children to use. Constructing the toys frequently calls for the use of sharp tools such as scissors, knives, awls, etc., which

are not safe for children to use. Throughout the book,
items which may be unsafe for young children to use are
noted with an asterisk (*). If your children help in
making toys, please be careful about possible hazards and
supervise the handling of tools very carefully. Do not
leave sharp tools lying around unattended where children
can get into them if you are called away during the
construction process.

CARDBORD BOXES/
CARDBOARD TUBES

Banjo

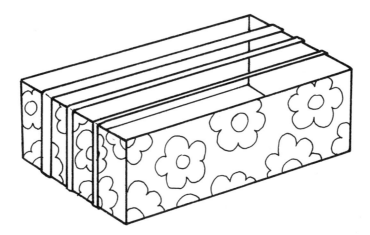

HOW TO USE IT

Add to a rhythm band collection for children to strum during a music activity time or use independently to accompany records or tapes. Can be used as a prop in dramatic play as "rock groups" or in talent show presentations for older preschoolers or school-age children. For added interest, set up a recording studio play area.

By varying size of boxes and rubber bands, call attention to the sounds produced by the different thicknesses and combinations of rubber bands and boxes (high and low), and to the rhythmic patterns (fast, slow) of the music.

WHAT IT DOES

Enhances enjoyment and appreciation of music. Provides children a means of actively participating in musical activity, and creating their own music. Focuses attention on some of the basic elements of music such as tempo, rhythm, pitch, quality of sound, etc. Also offers a way of experimenting with what factors help produce sound (vibration, tautness of string, thickness of string, size of open cavity, etc.). Also observe that the way the "banjo" is played can change the sound (i. e., strumming vs. plucking). Use of the "banjo" can help teach words such as high, low, fast, slow, resonance, vibration, pluck and strum.

WHAT YOU NEED TO MAKE IT

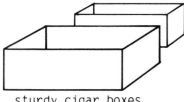
sturdy cigar boxes
(various sizes)

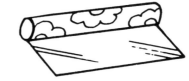
colorful contact paper

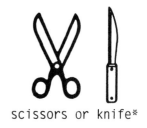
scissors or knife*

rubber bands, different
sizes and thicknesses

damp cloth

HOW TO MAKE IT

1. Wipe out cigar box and remove lid.

2. Cover sides of box with colorful contact paper.

3. Select 3-6 rubber bands of different thickness and stretch them around the box so they are parallel with its longer dimension.

4. Arrange rubber bands in sequence according to thickness from thin to thick (high to low sounds).

Shoe Box Train

HOW TO USE IT

Toddlers use the homemade train as a pull toy. They also enjoy putting their toys and stuffed animals into the boxes and using them to fill and dump. Encourage toddlers to take the toys for a ride and to talk about what they are doing.

Preschool children can make their own trains and use them to dramatize stories such as "The Little Engine that Could" or to set up a railroad yard and station dramatic play area.

WHAT IT DOES

Gives toddlers the chance to help create a toy they can then use in play. Let them color and decorate the boxes and observe as they are assembled into the train. They may imitate the process with other boxes. Gives them ideas for imaginative play. Talking about trains and how they are used stimulates language development. Read stories about trains and encourage children to use the train to retell the story.

WHAT YOU NEED TO MAKE IT

shoe boxes of various sizes

yarn or string

small pieces
of straws

a large button

markers

cut paper circles

glue

brass fasteners
(optional)

scissors*

HOW TO MAKE IT

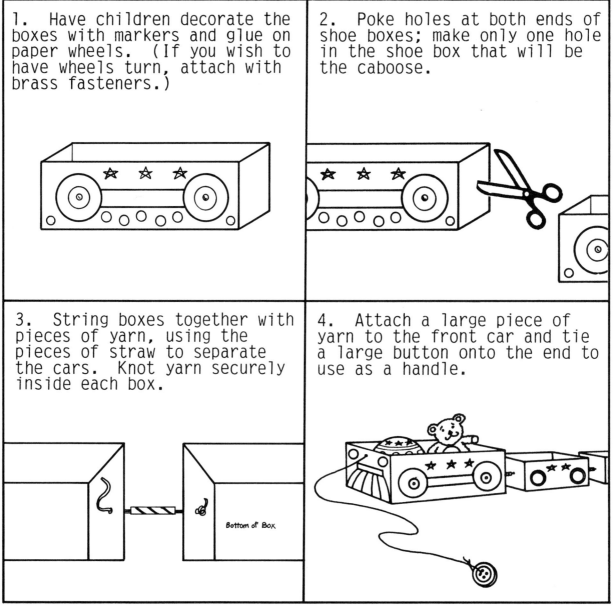

1. Have children decorate the boxes with markers and glue on paper wheels. (If you wish to have wheels turn, attach with brass fasteners.)

2. Poke holes at both ends of shoe boxes; make only one hole in the shoe box that will be the caboose.

3. String boxes together with pieces of yarn, using the pieces of straw to separate the cars. Knot yarn securely inside each box.

Bottom of Box

4. Attach a large piece of yarn to the front car and tie a large button onto the end to use as a handle.

Sizzling Rockets

HOW TO USE IT

Adults assemble materials needed to make these (see list and directions) and assist children as needed. Older preschoolers and school-age children can make these as a craft activity related to learning about rockets or for experimenting with air, motion and flight. Children can whirl them around in the air (inside or outside) and watch their rocket sparkle and flash its sizzling tails as it whirls around.

WHAT IT DOES

Provides a fun craft activity to make and use in a unit on rockets as a sample of a type of flying object. Craft activities provide practice in small motor and eye-hand coordination, following directions and completing a task. Encourages talking about rockets and discussing parts, construction, shape and appearance. Provides opportunity to observe how air works and affects this "rocket" as it moves through the air.

WHAT YOU NEED TO MAKE IT

cardboard tubes from
bathroom tissue

5" square piece of silver
paper or lightweight
aluminum foil

5"-long strips of silver
paper or foil (6-8 pieces)

2' piece of yarn or string   cellophane tape   stapler

HOW TO MAKE IT

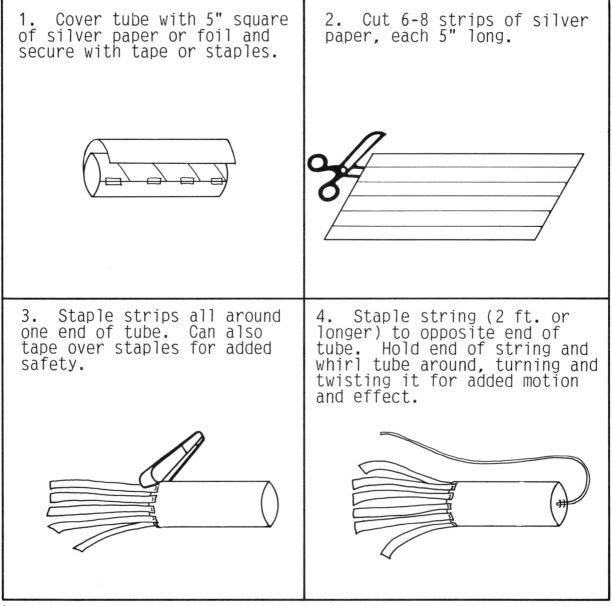

1. Cover tube with 5" square of silver paper or foil and secure with tape or staples.

2. Cut 6-8 strips of silver paper, each 5" long.

3. Staple strips all around one end of tube. Can also tape over staples for added safety.

4. Staple string (2 ft. or longer) to opposite end of tube. Hold end of string and whirl tube around, turning and twisting it for added motion and effect.

Tape Tube Animals

HOW TO USE IT

Make a variety of animals as a craft activity for school-age children and older preschoolers, or in connection with projects or units about animals. For young preschoolers, use in a table display about specific animals (i.e. pets, farm, zoo, etc.). Prepare materials needed to make the animals in advance and set out on a table. Show the children some pictures of animals, calling attention to special characteristics. Also show directions for putting these animals together, explaining the steps so they can make their own. Be available to assist as needed and discuss their animals. How can you tell the animals apart? Are they realistic or imaginary? Encourage children to paint or decorate them as they wish.

WHAT IT DOES

Provides an opportunity for children to learn something about the structure of animals and their specific identifying characteristics (i.e., bunny's pointy ears, puffy tail; duck's wings, webbed feet, bill; elephant's trunk, large ears, small tail, etc.). Provides practice in tracing, cutting, gluing, following directions and task completion. Can be used to stimulate discussion about types of animals and to create imaginative play with pretend animals.

WHAT YOU NEED TO MAKE IT

assorted cardboard
rings from rolls of
masking tape

scissors*

glue

construction paper

pencils

scraps of felt,
tagboard, etc.

paints (optional)

cotton balls

HOW TO MAKE IT

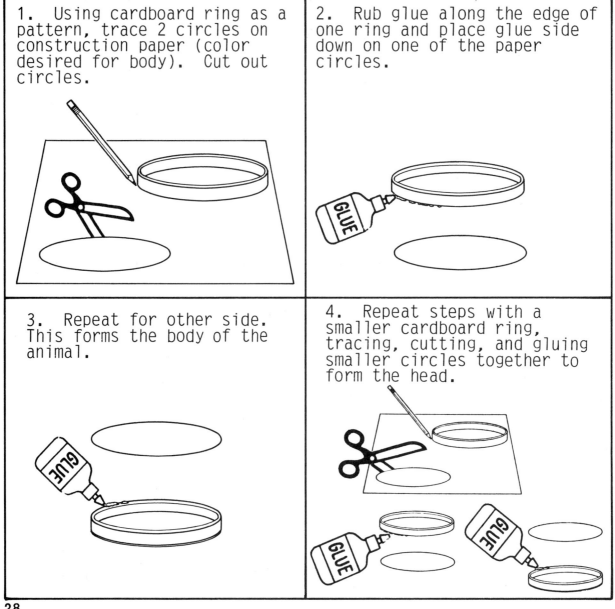

1. Using cardboard ring as a pattern, trace 2 circles on construction paper (color desired for body). Cut out circles.

2. Rub glue along the edge of one ring and place glue side down on one of the paper circles.

3. Repeat for other side. This forms the body of the animal.

4. Repeat steps with a smaller cardboard ring, tracing, cutting, and gluing smaller circles together to form the head.

5. Glue the head and body rings together. Hold for a few minutes to set; put down and let dry.

6. Cut body part shapes of tagboard or felt scraps. Glue to animal as appropriate. Decorate or paint as desired.

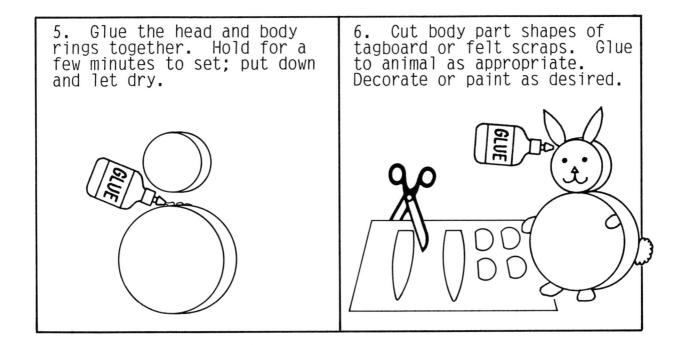

Top the Box

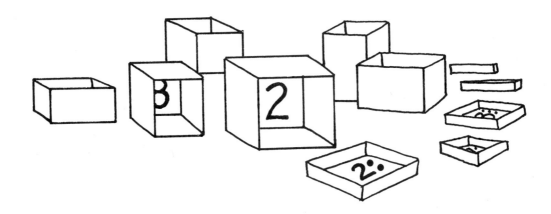

HOW TO USE IT

This is an independent activity in which one or two children try to find the number sets that go together. Spread out boxes in random fashion so the tops and bottoms are visible. The boxes should be different enough in dimensions so that each top fits only one bottom, making the game self-correcting. After matching the correct bottoms and tops, children may put the indicated number of small beads or pegs in each box.

Variation: Mount colors inside the bottoms and lids and let the children match the colors. Can also use boxes to sort beads by color.

WHAT IT DOES

Helps children learn to recognize numerals and what quantity each numeral represents. Also provides practice in fine motor skills in putting boxes together and perceptual skills in recognizing and matching sizes. Use to talk about the language concepts open, close, inside, top and bottom.

WHAT YOU NEED TO MAKE IT

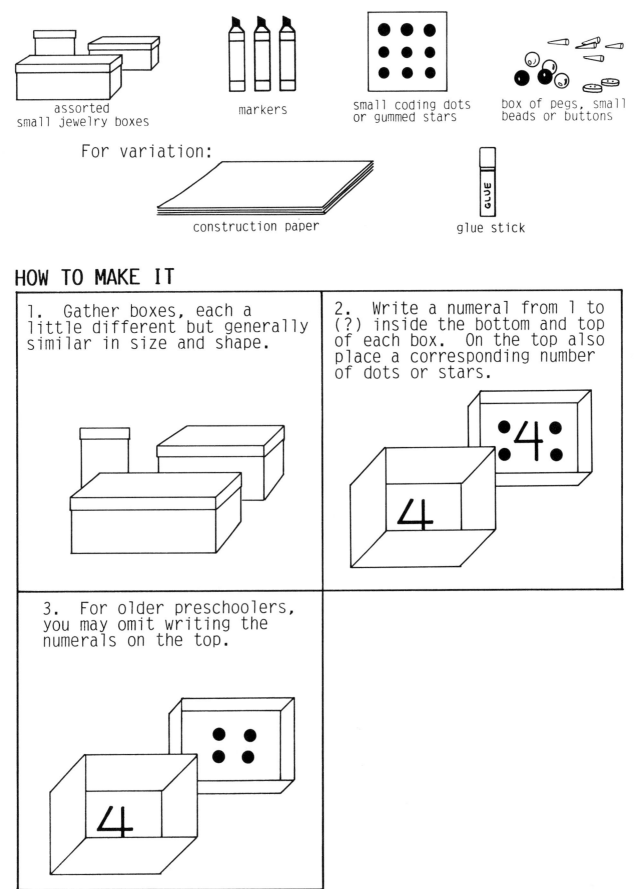

assorted
small jewelry boxes

markers

small coding dots
or gummed stars

box of pegs, small
beads or buttons

For variation:

construction paper

GLUE

glue stick

HOW TO MAKE IT

1. Gather boxes, each a little different but generally similar in size and shape.

2. Write a numeral from 1 to (?) inside the bottom and top of each box. On the top also place a corresponding number of dots or stars.

3. For older preschoolers, you may omit writing the numerals on the top.

Tube Puppet Playmates

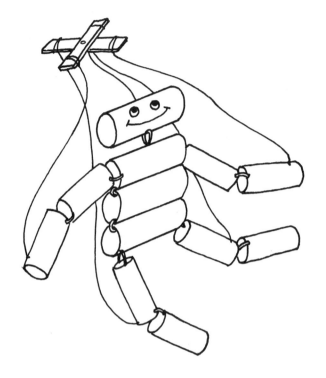

HOW TO USE IT

A fun prop to use in dramatic play. Tube characters can become familiar occupation figures such as fire fighters, doctors or other characters in dramatic play. Create animal tube characters for a pretend visit to a zoo or pet store. Use in preparation for or after a field trip.

Puppets can become characters in familiar stories to act out or retell the story or to put on puppet shows adapted from the story. Use puppets to talk about feelings. Can also be used to dramatize typical conflict situations and suggest ways to resolve them.

WHAT IT DOES

Stimulates and encourages imaginative play and language development. Provides a large-size "friend" to play with or use to help act out "scary" situations. Tube characters are easier to tell what to do and control than either other children or adults. Children can get mad at them without fear of consequences. Provides a means of extending and enhancing learning from field trips and stories. Provides practice in manipulating a puppet and fun in making arms and legs move.

WHAT YOU NEED TO MAKE IT

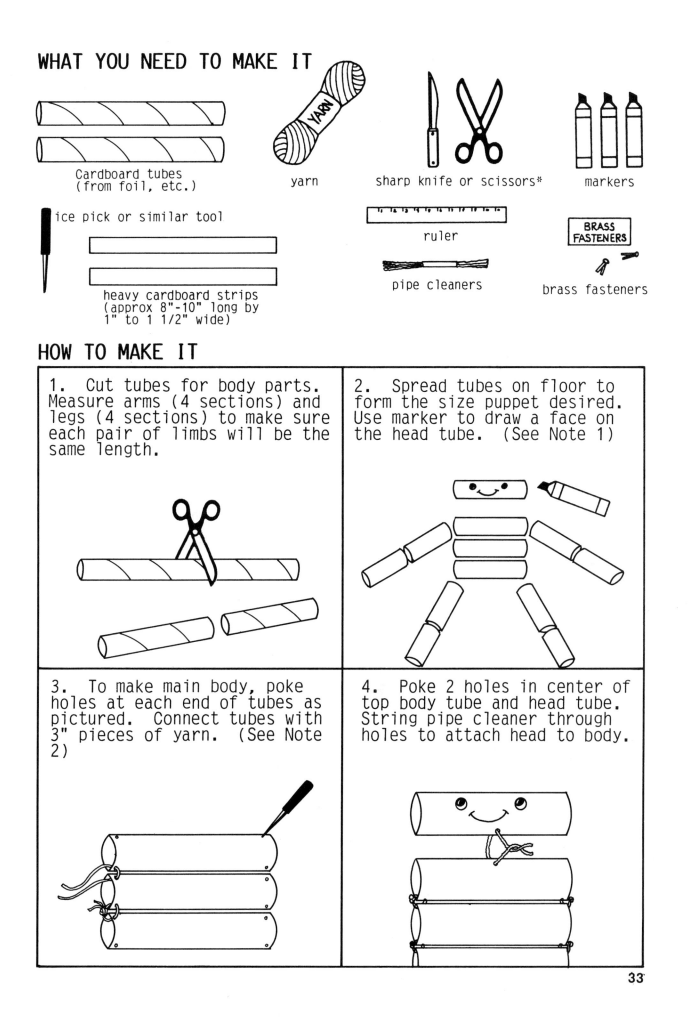

Cardboard tubes
(from foil, etc.)

yarn

sharp knife or scissors*

markers

ice pick or similar tool

heavy cardboard strips
(approx 8"-10" long by
1" to 1 1/2" wide)

ruler

pipe cleaners

BRASS
FASTENERS

brass fasteners

HOW TO MAKE IT

1. Cut tubes for body parts. Measure arms (4 sections) and legs (4 sections) to make sure each pair of limbs will be the same length.

2. Spread tubes on floor to form the size puppet desired. Use marker to draw a face on the head tube. (See Note 1)

3. To make main body, poke holes at each end of tubes as pictured. Connect tubes with 3" pieces of yarn. (See Note 2)

4. Poke 2 holes in center of top body tube and head tube. String pipe cleaner through holes to attach head to body.

5.   Assemble rest of puppet. Tie together limb sections and tie limbs to main body.

6.   Poke holes at lower end of arms, middle of legs, and center of head. Cut 5 long pieces of yarn and tie through those holes (puppet strings).

7.   Attach strips of cardboard together in center with brass fastener so they form a "t".

8.   Wrap puppet strings from limbs around ends of "t" leaving equal lengths running to arms and legs. Attach head string to brass fasteners in "t".

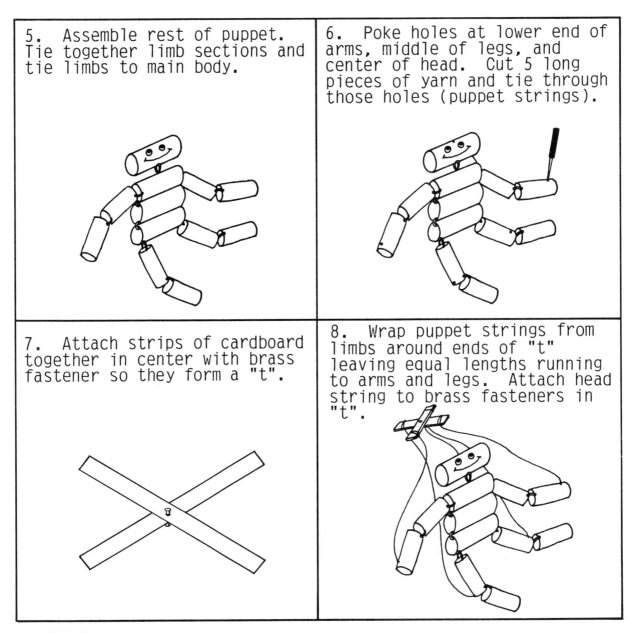

NOTES:

1.   Use 3-5 tubes for body, 1 for head, 2 sections each for arms and legs. Lay entire puppet out before poking holes to see where sections should be tied together.

2.   String can be used instead of yarn for construction.

CLOTH

Child Size Game Net

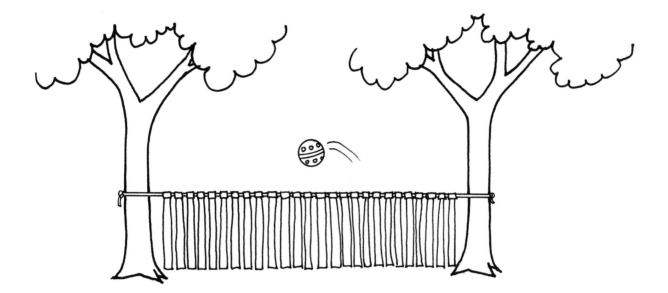

HOW TO USE IT

Can be used indoors or out and adjusted to children's interest, size and throwing abilities. Start with the net at or slightly above the children's height.

Indoors, string the net between two doorknobs, chairs, railings, etc. Outdoors, string between two trees (attach hooks to trees), outdoor equipment posts, etc.

Be sure you have an open playing area on either side of net, free of objects children could trip over. Two or more children throw or bat balls back and forth over net using hands. Large "soft" balls (beach, Nerf, etc.) work best. Also try balloons, badminton birdie or yarn balls with some kind of paddle (see Stocking Paddle in Teachables from Trashables).

WHAT IT DOES

Encourages cooperative play with others and also introduces simplified game playing concepts, rules, techniques (throwing balls over the net, rolling under the net, batting with palms, bouncing and hitting with paddle, etc.). Adults can introduce some ideas and procedures for play and let children practice and develop them in their own way. Back-and-forth game procedures provide practice in judging distance and speed as well as in taking turns. Also helps eye-hand coordination and development of throwing and catching skills.

WHAT YOU NEED TO MAKE IT

3 yards of
1/2" or 3/4"
elastic

old torn colorful sheets or
crepe paper streamers
cut to 30" strips

yardstick

scissors*

NOTE: Nets can be made any size to suit your play area and number of children. Net described is about 10' long when extended and hung. Use thin elastic for crepe paper, heavier elastic for cloth.

HOW TO MAKE IT

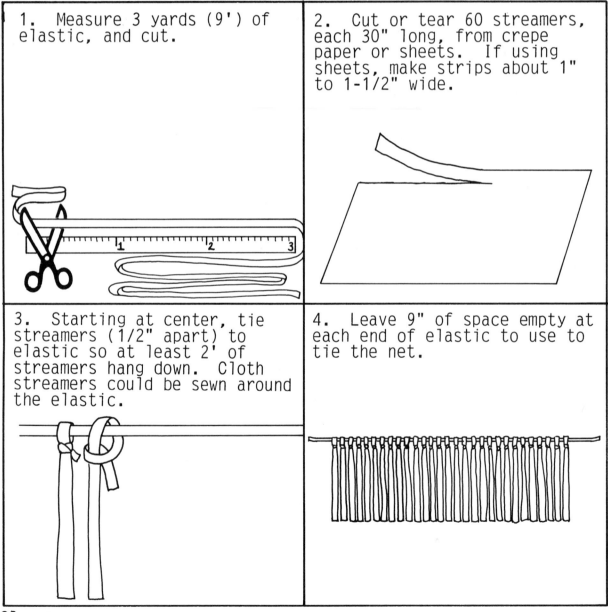

1. Measure 3 yards (9') of elastic, and cut.

2. Cut or tear 60 streamers, each 30" long, from crepe paper or sheets. If using sheets, make strips about 1" to 1-1/2" wide.

3. Starting at center, tie streamers (1/2" apart) to elastic so at least 2' of streamers hang down. Cloth streamers could be sewn around the elastic.

4. Leave 9" of space empty at each end of elastic to use to tie the net.

Furry Animal Friend

HOW TO USE IT

School-age children can make these and use as gifts for siblings, friends, or themselves. Can be used as props in dramatic play--i.e. several bears can be used to have a Teddy Bears' Picnic or to act out the Three Bears story or other favorite bear tales. Each child can have one as a nap toy or to take home and keep.

WHAT IT DOES

Gives each child a homemade replica of a favorite stuffed toy. Ideal to give as a holiday or end-of-the-year gift to the children. Good for parent involvement since you may want parents to help collect pictures for the stuffed animals, and you can give them an explanation of how you made them. Serves as a good model of making and using homemade toys.

WHAT YOU NEED TO MAKE IT

clear contact paper

fake fur

a plastic bag
(approximately

same size as picture)

COTTON
BATTING

cotton batting or foam
pieces for stuffing

stapler*

scissors*

a picture, approximately
8 1/2" x 11", of a
favorite animal toy

HOW TO MAKE IT

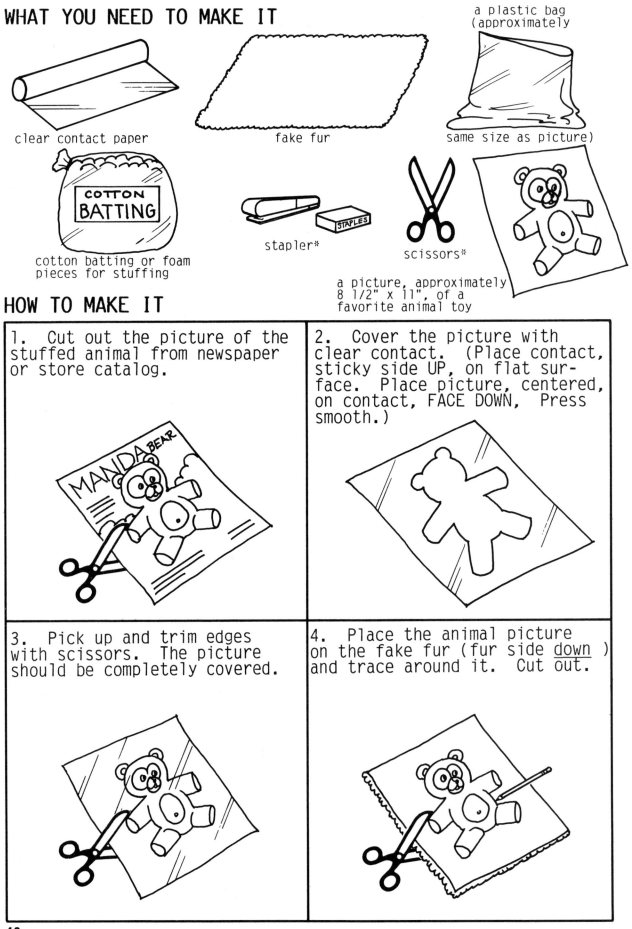

1. Cut out the picture of the stuffed animal from newspaper or store catalog.

MANDA BEAR

2. Cover the picture with clear contact. (Place contact, sticky side UP, on flat surface. Place picture, centered, on contact, FACE DOWN, Press smooth.)

3. Pick up and trim edges with scissors. The picture should be completely covered.

4. Place the animal picture on the fake fur (fur side <u>down</u>) and trace around it. Cut <u>out</u>.

5. Stuff cotton batting or foam pieces into the plastic bag. Fill to approximately 1 1/2" thick.

6. Put the three pieces together. Animal picture on one side, fur cutout (fur side out) on the other. Stuffed bag in the middle.

7. Staple or sew around edges. If made for toddlers, be sure to sew edges as staples can be pulled out. School-agers, however, enjoy   using and will be more successful with the stapler.

PLEASE NOTE: Putting the stuffing in a plastic bag makes the assembly process much easier. When assembled you should have a 1/2 furry friend that resembles the favorite toy because of the picture-perfect front!

Pillow Case Counters

HOW TO USE IT

Children put pillow cases on with number side in front. This is now "their number" to be used in playing games.
1. "7-up" (adult calls number and all children wearing that number stand up).
2. Children collect correct number of beads or blocks and put into their pockets.
3. With numbers on floor or chairs, children stand or sit on their number.
4. Play musical chairs; children find their spot when the music stops.

Can be used for organizing activities such as all children with same number sit at same table, or play in same activity area. Children can line their numbers up for practice in counting or for learning the numerical sequence.

WHAT IT DOES

Helps children become familiar with shapes of numbers so they can quickly identify them. Helps with number recognition and understanding that each number represents a specific quantity or set of objects. Provides concrete experience and practice with 1-to-1 number correspondence, an important pre-math concept. Initiates talk about numbers and offers a game approach for learning about them. Builds a learning experience based on children's enjoyment of putting things in their pockets.

WHAT YOU NEED TO MAKE IT

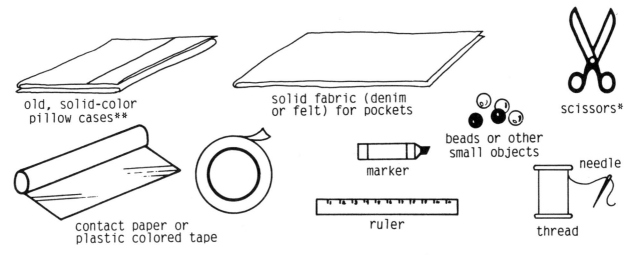

old, solid-color
pillow cases**

solid fabric (denim
or felt) for pockets

beads or other
small objects

scissors*

contact paper or
plastic colored tape

marker

ruler

needle

thread

HOW TO MAKE IT

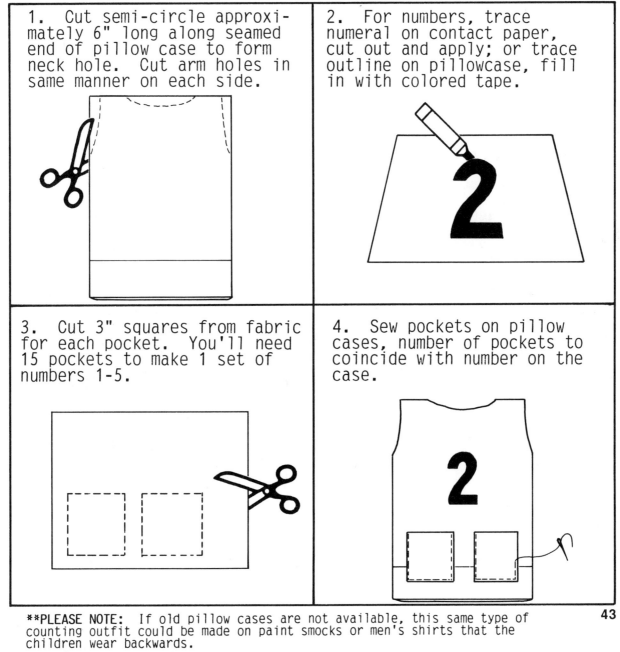

1. Cut semi-circle approximately 6" long along seamed end of pillow case to form neck hole. Cut arm holes in same manner on each side.

2. For numbers, trace numeral on contact paper, cut out and apply; or trace outline on pillowcase, fill in with colored tape.

3. Cut 3" squares from fabric for each pocket. You'll need 15 pockets to make 1 set of numbers 1-5.

4. Sew pockets on pillow cases, number of pockets to coincide with number on the case.

**PLEASE NOTE: If old pillow cases are not available, this same type of counting outfit could be made on paint smocks or men's shirts that the children wear backwards.

43

Quick & Easy Doll Clothes

HOW TO USE IT

The clothes can be used for dressing and undressing dolls. Practice mix-and-match outfits from various colored socks. The socks are easy for the children to pull on and off because they stretch and no buttons are involved. Children also like to wash the clothes and use clothespins to hang them on lines to dry. School-age children can make the clothes themselves. Various size clothes can be made by using a variety of sock sizes. They really stretch so even small socks can make usable outfits for small dolls.

WHAT IT DOES

Provides practice in dressing through pulling clothes on and off, and fitting arms and legs into appropriate holes. Teaches how to dress and undress a doll. Can be used to demonstrate matching outfits using all 3 pieces from the same sock or mixing colors that look good and matching part of the outfit (i.e. hats and pants). Can be used to teach about the care of clothes, washing, folding, etc. Using clothespins provides practice in fine motor control (thumb-fingers).

WHAT YOU NEED TO MAKE IT

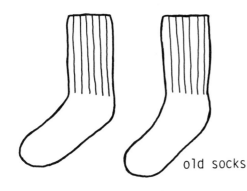

old socks

thread   needle

scissors*

HOW TO MAKE IT

1. Lay sock out and cut in thirds separating the toe section, the middle heel portion and the top.

←CUT

←CUT

2. Use the top of the sock for a dress or shirt and cut out arm holes on either side.

CUT →   ← CUT

3. In mid-section, sew a small closing in the middle of one end to provide separation for legs. (For long pants, cut and sew in an arch shape.)

4. The toe of the sock makes a hat, folding up to open edge.

Ring Around the Baby

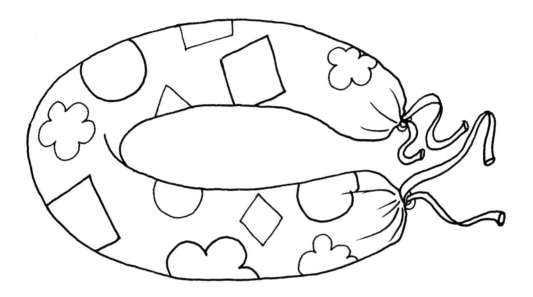

HOW TO USE IT

Place baby in center of ring with his/her buttocks on floor and upper body propped on the ring. Adjust the ring to baby's size and tie cords together so baby is secure in center.

Place in an area where toys can be suspended in front so baby can reach and grasp them. This semi-propped position leaves baby's hands free for play. Help baby feel the textured appliques on the ring surface.

WHAT IT DOES

Provides support for baby learning to sit up alone. A comfortable cushion for propping baby in a more upright position and providing a different view of things. Also serves to protect baby from other children accidentally bumping him/her. Allows the baby to see what's going on and provides sensory and tactile stimulation.

WHAT YOU NEED TO MAKE IT

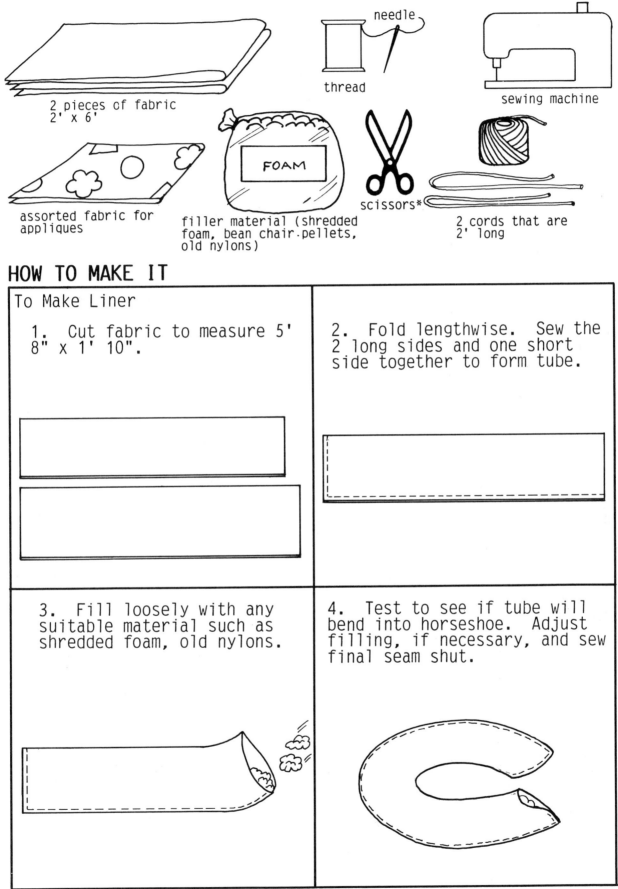

2 pieces of fabric
2' x 6'

needle

thread

sewing machine

assorted fabric for
appliques

FOAM

filler material (shredded
foam, bean chair pellets,
old nylons)

scissors*

2 cords that are
2' long

HOW TO MAKE IT

To Make Liner

1. Cut fabric to measure 5' 8" x 1' 10".

2. Fold lengthwise. Sew the 2 long sides and one short side together to form tube.

3. Fill loosely with any suitable material such as shredded foam, old nylons.

4. Test to see if tube will bend into horseshoe. Adjust filling, if necessary, and sew final seam shut.

To Make Cover

5. On right side of second piece of fabric, apply appliques of various textures and shapes.

6. Fold lengthwise, stitch long side (leave 2" opening). Make casing at each end for cord.

7. Insert 2' cord into casing at each end.

8. Place filled liner inside cover.

9. Pull cords tight and tie at each end.

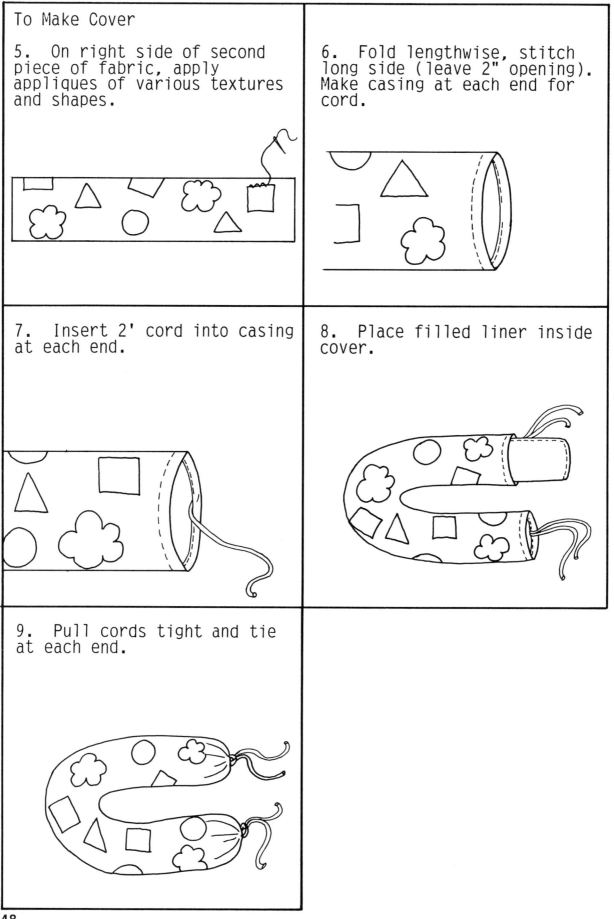

Take-Apart Teddy

HOW TO USE IT

Toddlers and young preschoolers enjoy taking the bear apart and sticking it back together again as well as putting decorative bows or clothes on the bear. Encourage toddlers to touch and talk about the textures and parts of the bear. Keep bear parts, bows and clothes together in a large plastic container or in a wicker basket for easy access.

Variation: Make other take-apart animals using patterns from pictures in coloring books. Separate head, limbs, tails, etc., from main body. Attach Velcro at appropriate spots for reassembly.

WHAT IT DOES

Encourages fine-motor development and thinking skills through "take-apart" and "put-together" activity. Provides tactile and sensory stimulation. Calls attention to animal body parts, how they fit together and what their names are.

Variation: Make different size bears and use for comparison. Use buttons or snaps instead of Velcro to teach those skills for 3 and 4 year olds.

WHAT YOU NEED TO MAKE IT

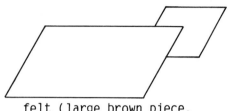

felt (large brown piece,
small colored pieces)

Velcro

fabric marker

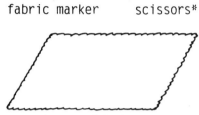

scissors*

pencil

needle and thread

fake fur or fabric scraps

HOW TO MAKE IT

1. Make copy of bear pattern (pg. 52) and trace onto brown felt.

2. Cut out felt pieces. Draw face on head piece with fabric marker.

3. Cut small pieces of Velcro. Sew on front of body and back of parts at dot marked (or use sticky-back Velcro patches).

4. Trace bow pattern on small pieces of colored felt or decorative fabric and cut out. Attach Velcro to back of bow. Make several different bows.

5.   Attach Velcro to bear body below head for bows. Add 2 or 3 other Velcro pieces below that.

6.   Cut several circles almost body size from fake fur scraps to use as clothes for bear. Attach Velcro to back.

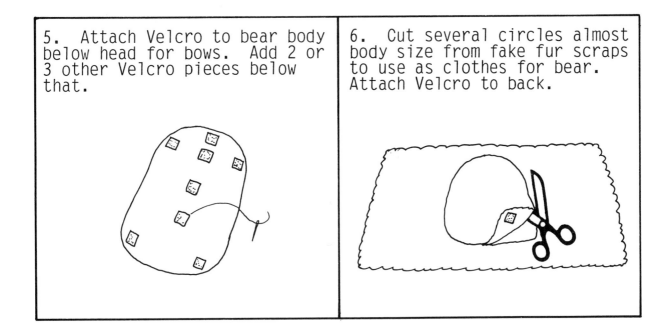

Position
Velcro on
reverse side
of areas
noted.

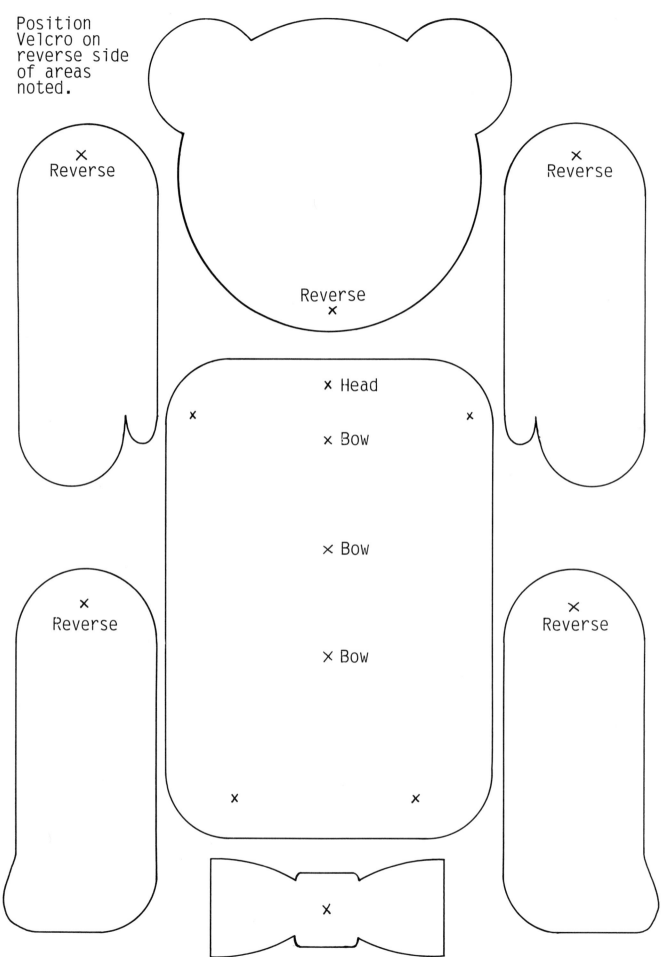

Reverse ×

Reverse ×

Reverse
×

× Head

× Bow

× Bow

× Bow

Reverse ×

Reverse ×

52

Target Toss

HOW TO USE IT

Demonstrate tossing balls gently at vest worn by a child or other adult. Explain how easily the ball sticks with a light toss and where the best place to aim would be (mid-area). Show how to remove ball by twisting it.

Have some children wear vests and others toss the Velcro-covered balls. Play dodgeball, having the ones with balls try to hit the moving targets. Tosses that miss can be picked up by any child and thrown again. When someone hits the "target", the vest is removed and the child who hit the target puts on that vest. Game continues until players (or adults) are tired of it.

WHAT IT DOES

Provides opportunity for children to follow directions and successfully participate in a simple non-threatening game. Helps children develop visual motor skills in an active way without fear of being hurt or failing. Strengthens eye-hand coordination and throwing skills as well as encouraging pre-catching skills. Children learn to watch ball as it moves in space and often move hands toward it as it reaches their vest.

WHAT YOU NEED TO MAKE IT

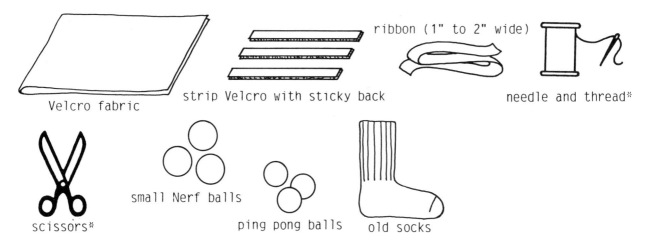

Velcro fabric

strip Velcro with sticky back

ribbon (1" to 2" wide)

needle and thread*

scissors*

small Nerf balls

ping pong balls

old socks

HOW TO MAKE IT

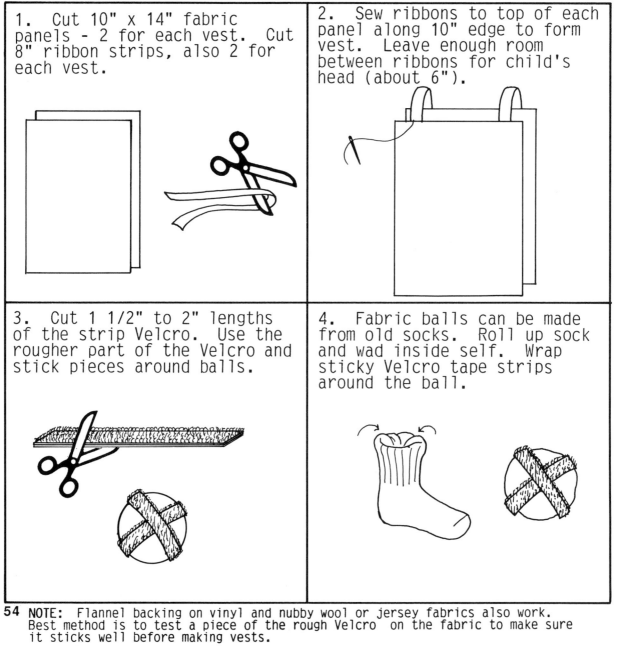

1. Cut 10" x 14" fabric panels - 2 for each vest. Cut 8" ribbon strips, also 2 for each vest.

2. Sew ribbons to top of each panel along 10" edge to form vest. Leave enough room between ribbons for child's head (about 6").

3. Cut 1 1/2" to 2" lengths of the strip Velcro. Use the rougher part of the Velcro and stick pieces around balls.

4. Fabric balls can be made from old socks. Roll up sock and wad inside self. Wrap sticky Velcro tape strips around the ball.

54 NOTE: Flannel backing on vinyl and nubby wool or jersey fabrics also work. Best method is to test a piece of the rough Velcro on the fabric to make sure it sticks well before making vests.

CLOTHESPINS

Child Safe Bulletin Board

HOW TO USE IT

Child pinches clothespin, inserts picture and releases pin. Use it to hang up children's art projects, paintings to dry or display, etc. Can also be used to display interesting pictures to look at and discuss. Look for stimulating or appealing pictures in magazines, calendars, brochures, advertisements, etc. Babies enjoy looking at pictures of faces and design patterns. Preschool age children can also use it to arrange pictures in a sequence to tell a story about something they have done or have learned about.

Can also be used as a mitten rack, smock holder, message holder or for any display purpose.

WHAT IT DOES

Provides an easy, safe and child-manageable way to display things and change them when desired. Children love being able to hang things up themselves and take them down again at will. Encourages independence and self-help as well as eye-hand coordination. Useful for all kinds of items from paintings to clothes. Using this for discussion of pictures and/or picture stories encourages language development, logical thinking and sequencing skills.

WHAT YOU NEED TO MAKE IT

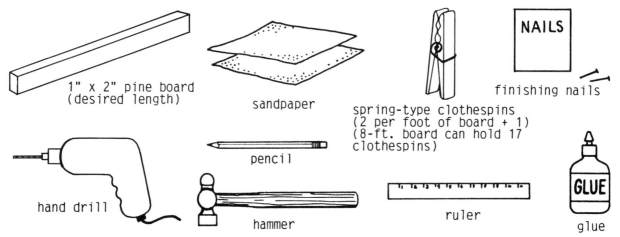

1" x 2" pine board
(desired length)

sandpaper

spring-type clothespins
(2 per foot of board + 1)
(8-ft. board can hold 17
clothespins)

NAILS

finishing nails

hand drill

pencil

hammer

ruler

GLUE

glue

HOW TO MAKE IT

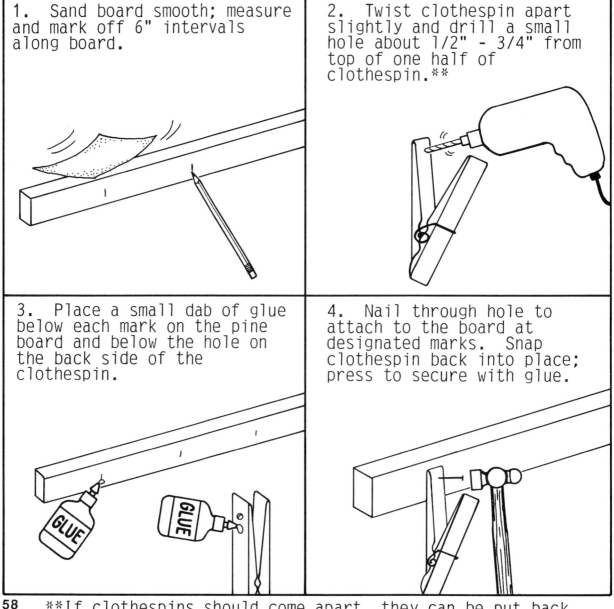

1. Sand board smooth; measure and mark off 6" intervals along board.

2. Twist clothespin apart slightly and drill a small hole about 1/2" - 3/4" from top of one half of clothespin.**

3. Place a small dab of glue below each mark on the pine board and below the hole on the back side of the clothespin.

4. Nail through hole to attach to the board at designated marks. Snap clothespin back into place; press to secure with glue.

58   **If clothespins should come apart, they can be put back together by snapping each half around the spring.

Instant Paintbrush

HOW TO USE IT

Attach clothespins to cut-up sponges. The clothespin becomes the handle of a paint brush which can be used at a table, easel or outdoors. Make a variety of different size and shape sponges for interesting effects. Let children wash sponges after use. Store in a covered container and keep on shelf ready to use.

Variation: For a variety of effects, also try using cotton balls, pieces of string, etc.

WHAT IT DOES

Provides an easy-to-make, low cost paint brush that is easier than many others for children to use. Makes painting less messy by keeping fingers out of the paint and encourages even reluctant painters to try. Turns any object, from feathers to leaves, into a paint brush. Encourages creativity and imagination in exploring and using new ideas and materials, as well as eye-hand coordination in assembling and using the brushes.

WHAT YOU NEED TO MAKE IT

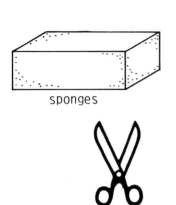

sponges

clip clothespins

tempera paint

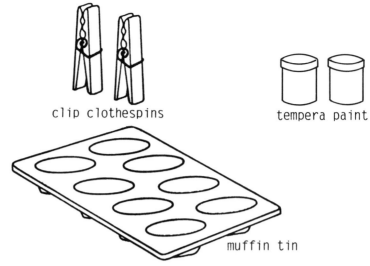

scissors*

muffin tin

HOW TO MAKE IT

1. Cut up sponges into 8 - 10 different shapes. Make a variety of sizes as well as shapes. Clip to clothespins.

2. Mix tempera paints with water (or use pre-mixed paints) and pour into muffin tin. Leave 2 or 3 cups empty to hold extra brushes.

NOTE: Paint may also be kept in small plastic containers with covers if desired.

Pizza Pin-Ups

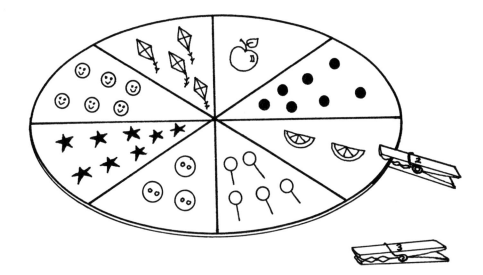

HOW TO USE IT

Can be used in a number activities interest area or as a small group or individual activity.

Tell the children to look at one "slice" (or section) of the pizza board and count how many pictures they see in it. Have one child find the clothespin with the matching number on it. If he/she is not sure of the number, turn the clothespin over and count the dots to see if the numbers match. Then clip that clothespin to the corresponding pizza slice. Continue until all the clothespins are attached. Children will be able to do this activity independently after being shown the procedure.

WHAT IT DOES

Helps children learn correct numerical value by giving them practice in counting and matching. Provides practice with the idea that each number stands for a corresponding quantity of items. Manipulating clothespins provides small-motor practice.

Variation: Can make similar games to match colors or letters.

WHAT YOU NEED TO MAKE IT

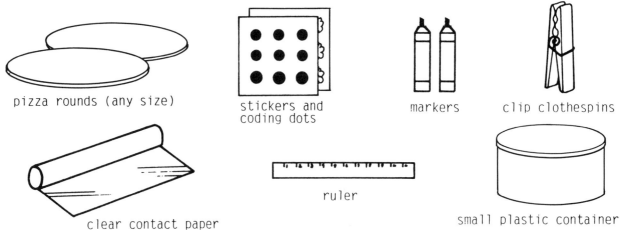

pizza rounds (any size)

stickers and coding dots

markers

clip clothespins

clear contact paper

ruler

small plastic container

HOW TO MAKE IT

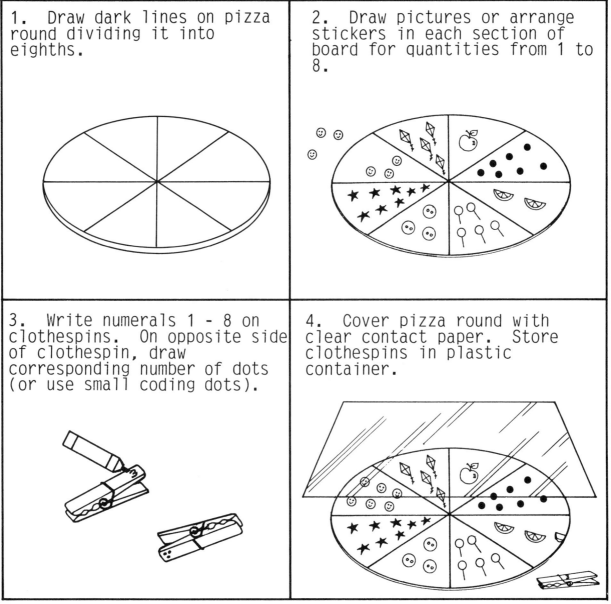

1. Draw dark lines on pizza round dividing it into eighths.

2. Draw pictures or arrange stickers in each section of board for quantities from 1 to 8.

3. Write numerals 1 - 8 on clothespins. On opposite side of clothespin, draw corresponding number of dots (or use small coding dots).

4. Cover pizza round with clear contact paper. Store clothespins in plastic container.

FILE FOLDERS/ TAGBOARD

Counting Circles

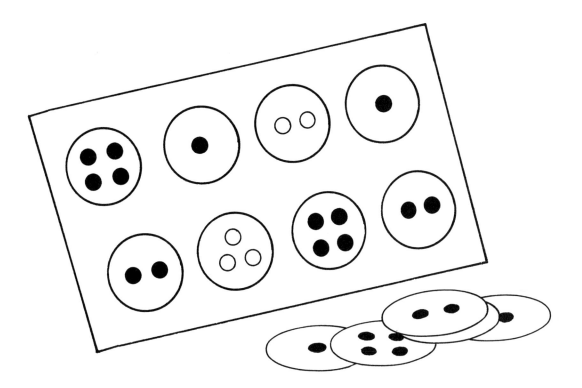

HOW TO USE IT

A number and color match game which is appropriate for individual or small group use. In small group game, place master board in center and deal playing cards around the group. Point to a circle on the master board and describe it by color and number (i.e.: "green 4's"). All children with those cards place them on the matching master board space. Alternate games can use a single category (i.e.: "all red", "all 2's"). Children with cards matching the category place them on the board.

WHAT IT DOES

Offers practice in comparing and matching sets of dots by number or color. Also helps children associate specific numerals with the corresponding quantity. With direction, helps illustrate number concept words such as more, less, many. Provides a simple game that encourages children to take turns and pay attention, along with playing and teaching number concepts.

WHAT YOU NEED TO MAKE IT

tagboard

1/2" coding dots in a
variety of colors

marker   3" circle pattern

clear contact

scisssors*

HOW TO MAKE IT

Master Playing Board

1. Using 8" x 16" tagboard, trace 2 rows of 3" diameter circles for master board.

2. Mount coding dots in circles, using different colors for each circle, but consistent dot arrangement for each number.

3. Cover master board with clear contact.

Playing Cards

4. On another piece of tagboard, trace circles as on playing board.

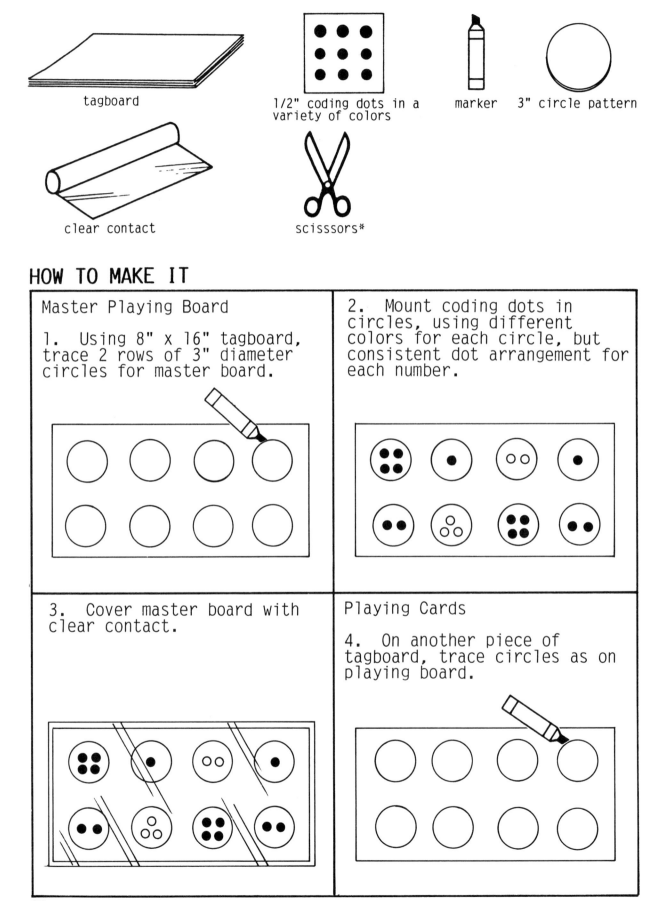

66

5. Place coding dots to match playing board. Write corresponding numeral on back of each if desired.

6. Cover cards with clear contact. Cut cards apart.

NOTES:

1. For younger children, write numeral in same color as dots. For older children, write numerals in black.

2. Make as many pieces as you wish since more than 1 circle can match the circle on the master board.

3. For larger group, or older children, enlarge master board and draw 20 circles. Increase number of playing cards as well.

Cube-It

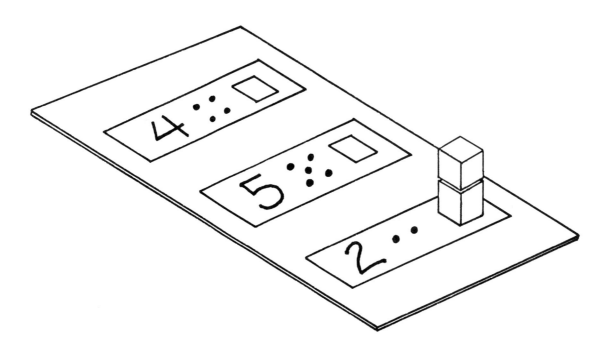

HOW TO USE IT

Can be used by 1 or 2 children as an independent activity. Child spreads out all the task cards and reads the numerals or counts the dots to determine the number and color of blocks needed to complete the task. For example, if number 4 has a red square, the child finds 4 red cubes and stacks them on that square. Variations for older children: Add a minute timer to see how quickly they can complete a card. Encourage children to count their stacks as they do them so they use the right quantity for each number.

WHAT IT DOES

Provides practice in counting objects from 1 to 10 and matching the correct amount to each numeral which teaches 1-to-1 number correspondence, a crucial step in understanding what numbers mean. Helps teach organizing by category, such as color. Emphasizes focusing on and completing a specific task. Using a timer introduces idea of completing a task quickly. Provides a new use for blocks. Uses simple reading and provides practice in working from left to right.

WHAT YOU NEED TO MAKE IT

tagboard sheets
(8" x 10")

black coding dots

marker

scissors*

clear contact

construction paper

ruler

color cubes (small blocks
or square beads)

HOW TO MAKE IT

1. Rule off 3 or 4 rectangle work spaces on tagboard and print a numeral in the left-hand side of each box.

| 4 |
| 5 |
| 2 |

2. Mount the corresponding number of dots next to each numeral. Leave zero empty.

| 4 :: |
| 5 ::: |
| 2 •• |

3. Cut 1" squares of construction paper in colors that match the color cubes that you have. Glue on the right hand side of each box.

| 4 :: □ |
| 5 ::: □ |
| 2 •• |

4. Cover counting boards with clear contact.

| 4 :: □ |
| 5 ::: □ |
| 2 •• □ |

Dots to Dinosaurs

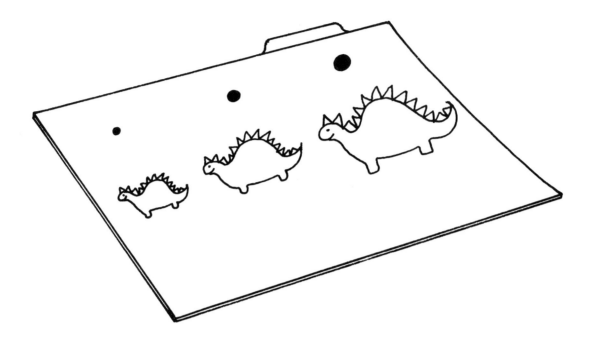

HOW TO USE IT

Children match the dinosaurs to the dots according to size. Have children find all the small dinosaurs and put them next to the smallest dot and then continue to the middle size and largest. Be sure to say the words "dots" and "dinosaurs". Can add other small, medium and large size pictures of things that begin with the D sound like dolls, ducks, dresses, dogs, etc.

WHAT IT DOES

Teaches auditory discrimination skills matching sounds for the letter D (dots, dinosaurs, and other "D" words). Sequencing by size encourages visual discrimination; matching letter sounds develops auditory skills.

This same type of game can be used with other letter sound discrimination by changing the cues and having pictures beginning with other sounds. For example, for "S", use "stars" (instead of dots) and match pictures of "shells".

WHAT YOU NEED TO MAKE IT

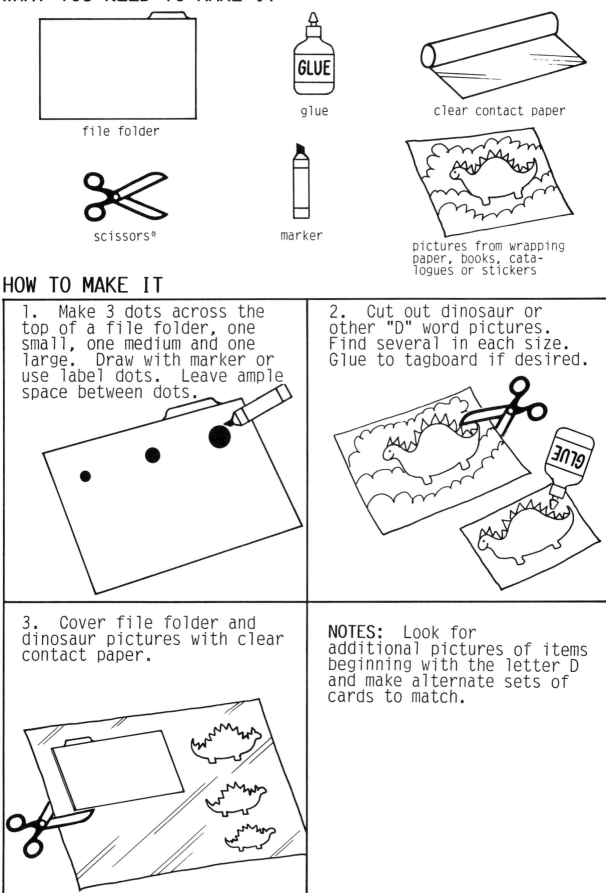

file folder

glue

clear contact paper

scissors*

marker

pictures from wrapping paper, books, catalogues or stickers

HOW TO MAKE IT

1. Make 3 dots across the top of a file folder, one small, one medium and one large. Draw with marker or use label dots. Leave ample space between dots.

2. Cut out dinosaur or other "D" word pictures. Find several in each size. Glue to tagboard if desired.

3. Cover file folder and dinosaur pictures with clear contact paper.

NOTES: Look for additional pictures of items beginning with the letter D and make alternate sets of cards to match.

Letter Line-Up

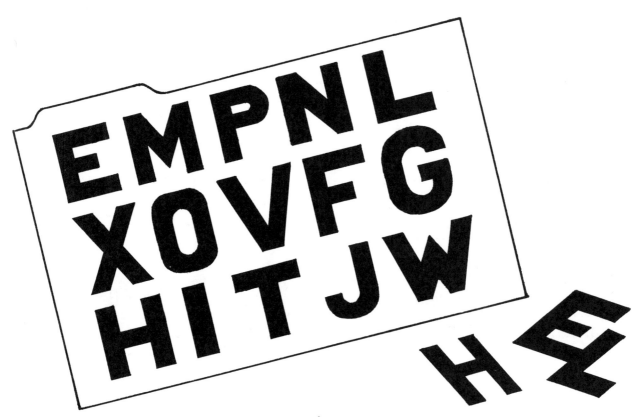

HOW TO USE IT

Children match the individual letters to the same one on the file folder. Can be used individually or as a small group game with each child taking a turn picking a letter to match. Can include more than 1 match for each letter.

Variation for older children: Add a set of cue cards with pictures on them. Children match the card to the letter associated with the initial sound of the object pictured (i.e., ball matched to letter B). Can have children think of words that begin with specific letter sounds.

WHAT IT DOES

Helps children become familiar with letters by playing with them and matching how they look. Teaches letter recognition and matching. The variations aid initial sound recognition, and word-letter associations. All of these visual and auditory discrimination tasks help children get ready to read.

WHAT YOU NEED TO MAKE IT

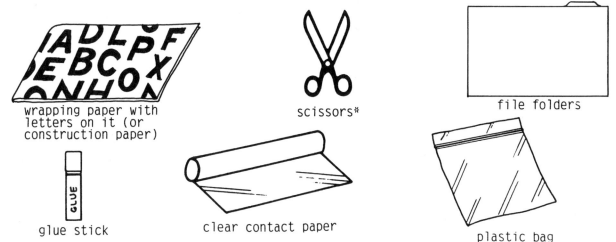

wrapping paper with letters on it (or construction paper)

scissors*

file folders

glue stick

clear contact paper

plastic bag

HOW TO MAKE IT

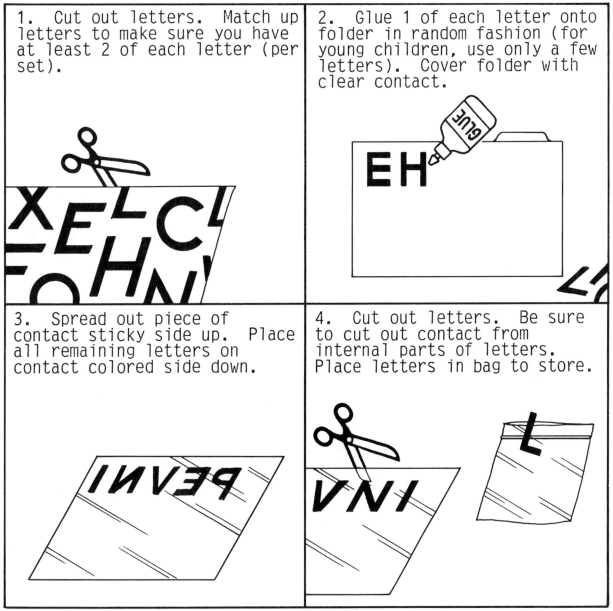

1. Cut out letters. Match up letters to make sure you have at least 2 of each letter (per set).

2. Glue 1 of each letter onto folder in random fashion (for young children, use only a few letters). Cover folder with clear contact.

3. Spread out piece of contact sticky side up. Place all remaining letters on contact colored side down.

4. Cut out letters. Be sure to cut out contact from internal parts of letters. Place letters in bag to store.

Money Matters

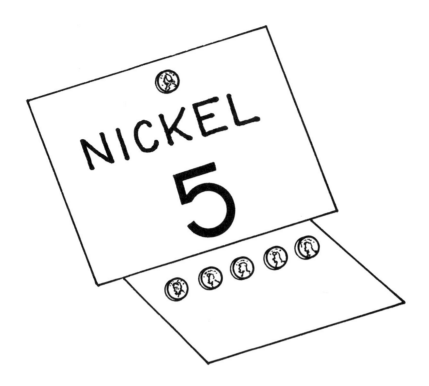

HOW TO USE IT

Children use it to count out and match amounts of play money or paper circles ("pennies") that each coin represents (i.e.: 5 circles equals nickel). Children can make play money by making rubbings of coins. Adults can use the cards to see if children recognize the value of specific coins. Hold the cards with numeral covered up (fold lower card over upper one) and see if child recognizes coin and can tell how many cents (or pennies) it is worth. Can also make extra sets of the small money cards. Use to demonstrate combinations for coin value. For example, make 5 cards with 5 pennies on them and a few with nickels and dimes to use in showing the different combinations that make 25 cents.

WHAT IT DOES

Teaches about the amounts or value represented in each of our coins. Helps illustrate which coins are worth more by providing practice in counting out the number of pennies in each coin. Teaches recognition of coins and the words we use for them. Good to use in a unit about banks or in studying about stores. For older children, teaches reading of words for coins, also provides practice in counting and number recognition since each coin also represents a numerical value. Recommended for children over 4.

WHAT YOU NEED TO MAKE IT

heavy tagboard,
4 pieces 6 1/2" x 7"
4 pieces 4 1/2" by 5"

42 pennies

1 quarter

1 dime

1 nickel

tape

scissors*

marker

glue

clear contact

crayon
for rubbing

paper

play money or
paper circle
coins

HOW TO MAKE IT

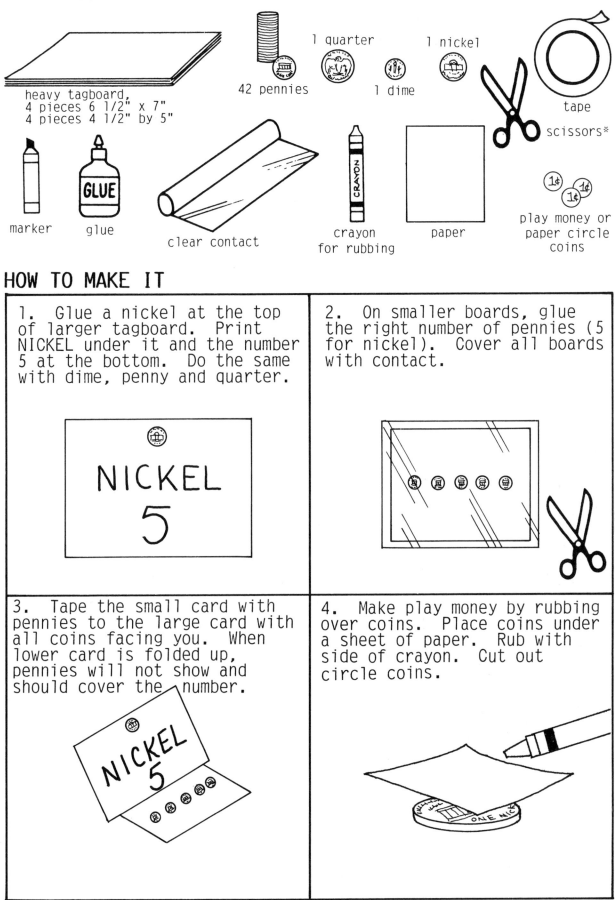

1. Glue a nickel at the top of larger tagboard. Print NICKEL under it and the number 5 at the bottom. Do the same with dime, penny and quarter.

NICKEL
5

2. On smaller boards, glue the right number of pennies (5 for nickel). Cover all boards with contact.

3. Tape the small card with pennies to the large card with all coins facing you. When lower card is folded up, pennies will not show and should cover the number.

NICKEL
5

4. Make play money by rubbing over coins. Place coins under a sheet of paper. Rub with side of crayon. Cut out circle coins.

Numbers Galore

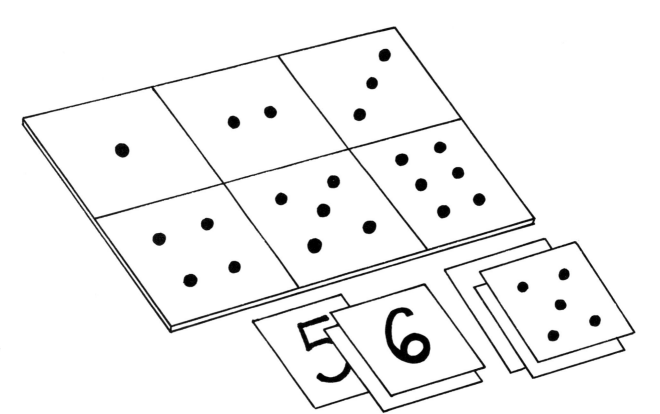

HOW TO USE IT

There are numerous games that can be played with these sets of cards.

1.) Non-competitive bingo: Four children each have a bingo board and counters. Leader calls number and children cover that number with a marker. Since all boards have same numbers on them, all children finish at same time.

2) Concentration: Cards placed face down and children find pairs that are the same. Can be played with either the small dot cards or the numerals.

3) Match-Ups: Dot cards to bingo boards; numeral cards to dot cards, etc.

WHAT IT DOES

Provides a game with many possible adaptations, encouraging adults and children to try out new ideas and illustrating how one item can be used in various ways. Teaches numeral recognition, matching like sets and matching numerals to the correct quantity. Encourages counting from 1 to 6. Introduces concept of number sets, i.e., 4 cards with 3 on them are a set of 3's. Encourages playing some games in non-competitive ways, allowing all players to par-participate simultaneously. Can also use in combination with counters or dice to make other matching or counting games.

WHAT YOU NEED TO MAKE IT

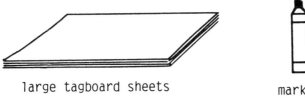

large tagboard sheets

marker

black coding dots

scissors*

clear contact

pencil

ruler

bingo markers

HOW TO MAKE IT

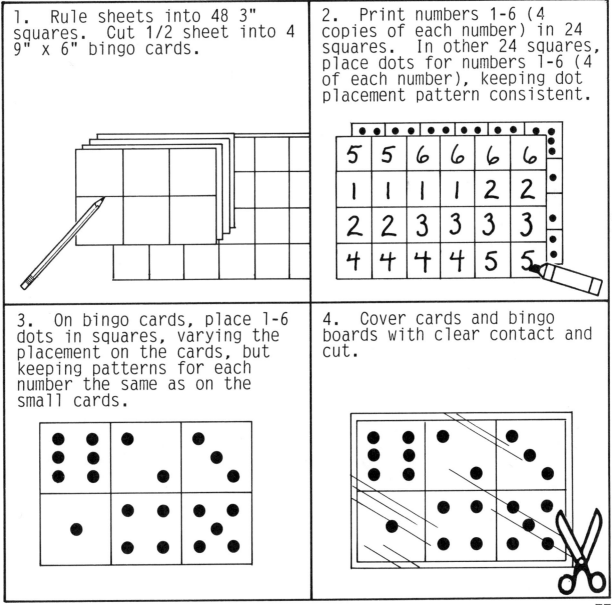

1. Rule sheets into 48 3" squares. Cut 1/2 sheet into 4 9" x 6" bingo cards.

2. Print numbers 1-6 (4 copies of each number) in 24 squares. In other 24 squares, place dots for numbers 1-6 (4 of each number), keeping dot placement pattern consistent.

5	5	6	6	6	6
1	1	1	1	2	2
2	2	3	3	3	3
4	4	4	4	5	5

3. On bingo cards, place 1-6 dots in squares, varying the placement on the cards, but keeping patterns for each number the same as on the small cards.

4. Cover cards and bingo boards with clear contact and cut.

Numerous Numerals

HOW TO USE IT

Can be played by 4 children.
Each child has a lotto card.
Leader picks a card from the
stack and identifies it by
color and number (i.e.: "Who
has the yellow 4?). The child
who has it on his lotto board
takes the card and covers the
matching numeral on his board.
Continue playing until all the
cards are given out.

Variation: A similar game can
be made with letters.

WHAT IT DOES

Provides a simple game-playing
activity that helps children
learn to recognize and match
numerals and identify number
words. Also teaches color
recognition and provides
experience in playing a small
group game, listening and
paying attention. The letter
variation games encourage
similar skills, with an empha-
sis on letter recognition,
matching and noticing likenesses and differences in
letter forms.

WHAT YOU NEED TO MAKE IT

tagboard

construction paper
(6 colors)

markers

scissors*

patterns or stencil for
numerals (if desired)

glue

clear contact

HOW TO MAKE IT

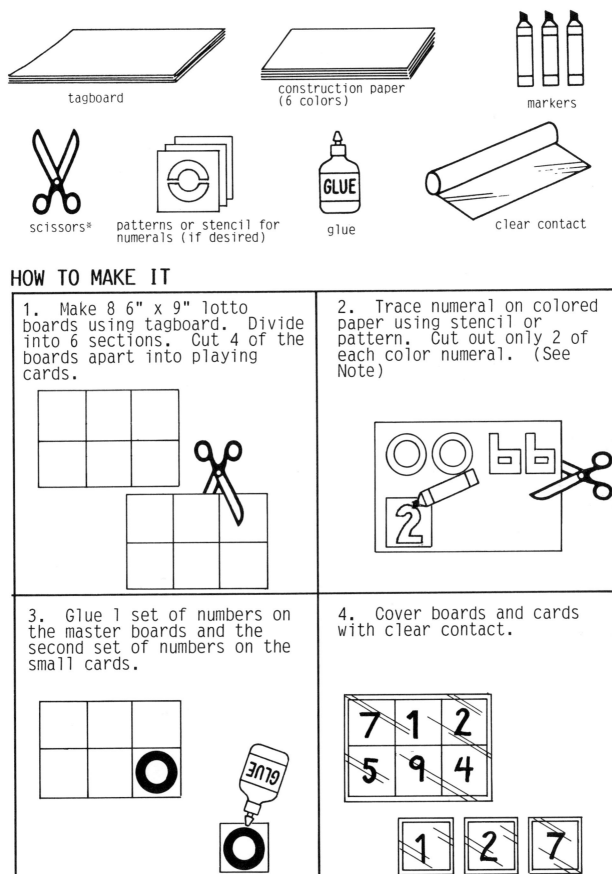

1. Make 8 6" x 9" lotto boards using tagboard. Divide into 6 sections. Cut 4 of the boards apart into playing cards.

2. Trace numeral on colored paper using stencil or pattern. Cut out only 2 of each color numeral. (See Note)

3. Glue 1 set of numbers on the master boards and the second set of numbers on the small cards.

4. Cover boards and cards with clear contact.

NOTE: You will need 24 pairs. A pair is 2 of the same numeral in the same color.

79

Painter's Palette

HOW TO USE IT

Store 3 or 4 color boards and the matching color pieces in a small wicker basket or box. Children spread out the color boards and find the smaller pieces to match each color. For young children, make boards with very different colors. As skill increases, make and use boards which require more precise color discrimination (i.e.: use different shades of one color). For older children, put out large boxes of crayons or colored pencils and paper and see if children can draw sets of shades of colors that match the sample boards. Integrate color boards into curriculum for holidays (i.e.: on Valentine's Day use red and pink) or "special days" (i.e.: Purple Day).

WHAT IT DOES

Provides practice in matching colors and learning to recognize different shades and tints of the same color. Helps to teach concepts of lighter and darker in relation to color concepts. Encourages visual perceptual skills through noticing and paying attention to small differences. Good to use in teaching about color since games can be made in varying shades of all colors.

WHAT YOU NEED TO MAKE IT

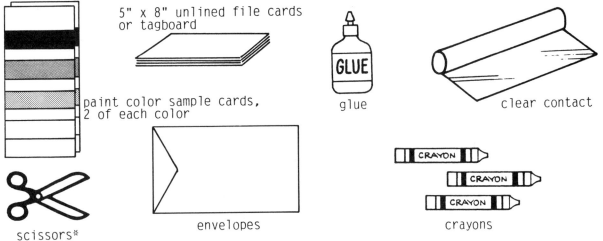

5" x 8" unlined file cards or tagboard

paint color sample cards, 2 of each color

glue

clear contact

scissors*

envelopes

crayons

HOW TO MAKE IT

1. Cut out the paint color samples. Be sure to have 2 of each color.

2. Select colors desired (either different or similar). Glue 1 set on file card. Leave second set in pieces.

3. Cover cards and pieces with clear contact.

4. Store cards and color samples in envelopes, divided by colors if desired.

Shape Finders

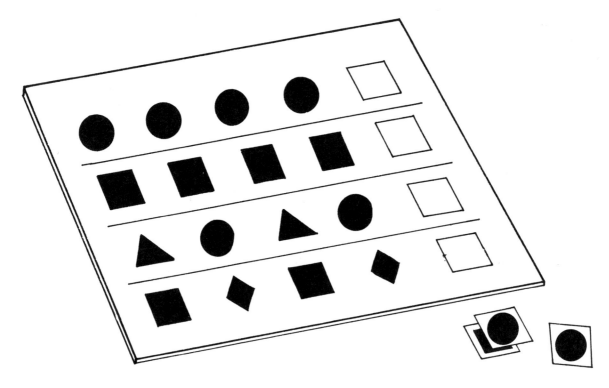

HOW TO USE IT

Child finds the small "shape" card that completes each sequence and places it in the "empty box" on the larger card. Can be used by one child as an independent activity or played by 2-4 children as a type of bingo game.

Instructions for "Bingo": Give players 1 or 2 larger game cards. Put all the smaller pieces in a pile. Children take turns picking the small cards and seeing who needs that card. An adult may want to serve as a caller or demonstrator the first few times the game is used. Continue playing until all cards are completed.

WHAT IT DOES

Helps the child learn to recognize a sequential pattern. Teaches color and shape recognition. Encourages problem solving and thinking skills in deciding what comes next. Teaches taking turns and cooperation in playing a game.

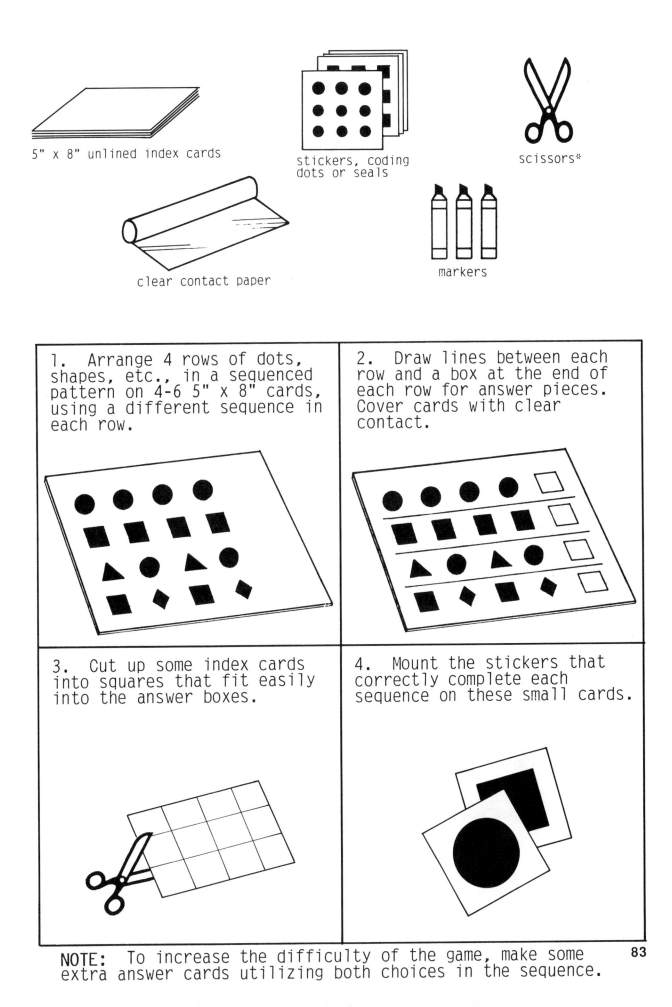

5" x 8" unlined index cards

stickers, coding dots or seals

scissors*

clear contact paper

markers

1. Arrange 4 rows of dots, shapes, etc., in a sequenced pattern on 4-6 5" x 8" cards, using a different sequence in each row.

2. Draw lines between each row and a box at the end of each row for answer pieces. Cover cards with clear contact.

3. Cut up some index cards into squares that fit easily into the answer boxes.

4. Mount the stickers that correctly complete each sequence on these small cards.

NOTE: To increase the difficulty of the game, make some extra answer cards utilizing both choices in the sequence.

Sociable Cracker Game

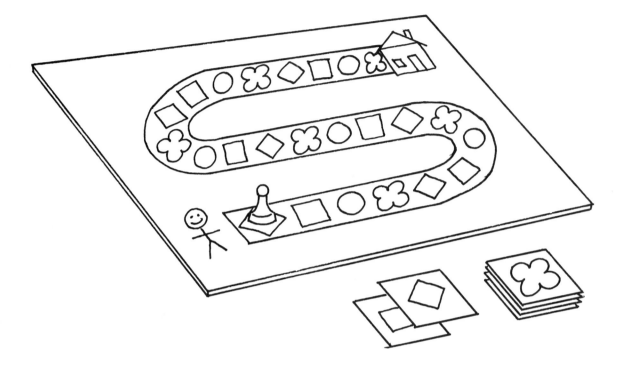

HOW TO USE IT

Can be used with both small and large groups of children for a variety of games. For a small group game: Place playing cards face down on table or floor. Children take turns drawing cards one at a time trying to match the next shape needed on the board (i.e., if a square is next on the board, child keeps drawing cards until a square is drawn). Cards are returned to the card pile after each turn. Next child draws until finding the next shape on path, and moves the marker. Each child, in turn, continues along path until marker reachs "home" place.

Variation: Can place crackers directly on board and children take turns at drawing cards to match next cracker shape to eat. With 6 players, each would get 4 crackers.

WHAT IT DOES

Helps develop awareness of shapes in common objects and encourages children to recognize likenesses and differences in shapes. Provides practice at turn-taking, playing a simple, non-competitive game, and following directions.

For a quick snack time game promoting social interaction, children draw cards, move to that shape space and choose a cracker to match. Make 1 game for each table.

84

WHAT YOU NEED TO MAKE IT

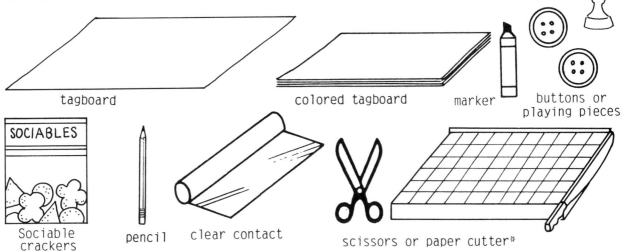

tagboard

colored tagboard

marker

buttons or playing pieces

SOCIABLES

Sociable crackers

pencil

clear contact

scissors or paper cutter*

HOW TO MAKE IT

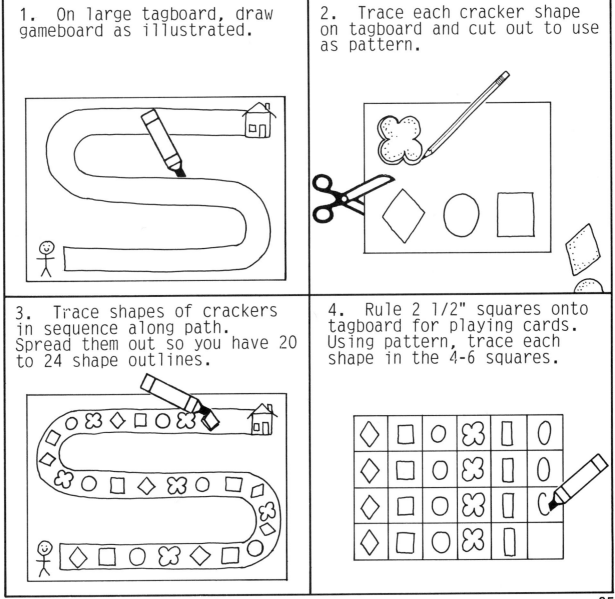

1.   On large tagboard, draw gameboard as illustrated.

2.   Trace each cracker shape on tagboard and cut out to use as pattern.

3.   Trace shapes of crackers in sequence along path. Spread them out so you have 20 to 24 shape outlines.

4.   Rule 2 1/2" squares onto tagboard for playing cards. Using pattern, trace each shape in the 4-6 squares.

5. Cover board and cards with clear contact. Cut cards apart.

Stop & Go Race Game

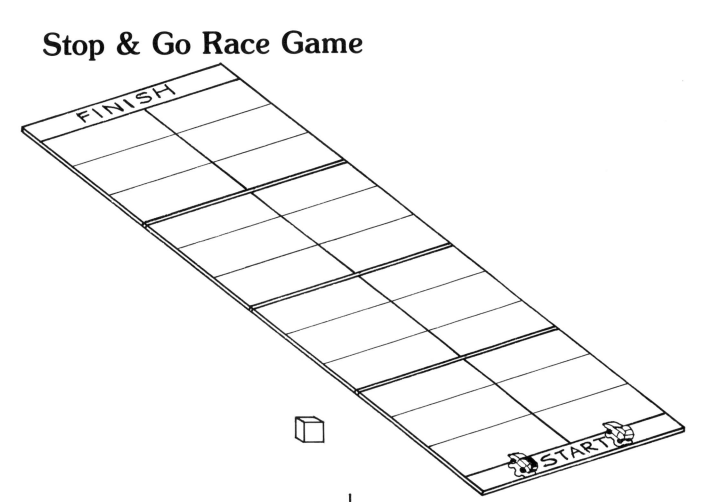

HOW TO USE IT

Game is played by two players who take turns shaking the cube (as dice) and moving their cars according to the cube's color. Red means stop; green means go.

Each child chooses a small car to use as his/her playing piece and places it on the car outline on the start line. When a player shakes a green, that player's car moves ahead one space; when a red shows, then the player's car does not move. Game ends when both cars have crossed the finish line. Cloth tape allows the board to fold easily for storage. Can use any size wooden cube or make one from milk cartons. (For directions, see Clock Matching, pg. 161.)

WHAT IT DOES

Helps teach children to associate "red" with stop and "green" with go. Good to use when teaching about traffic lights or transportation or as part of an interest center about cars, traffic or transportation. Since children love to play with small cars, this encourages them to use them cooperatively in a simple game and models the idea of making up new ways to use cars in play.

WHAT YOU NEED TO MAKE IT

4 sheets of tabgoard
8" x 11"

cloth tape

2" wooden cube

2 small cars

marker

ruler

paint brush

red and green paint

scissors*

clear contact

HOW TO MAKE IT

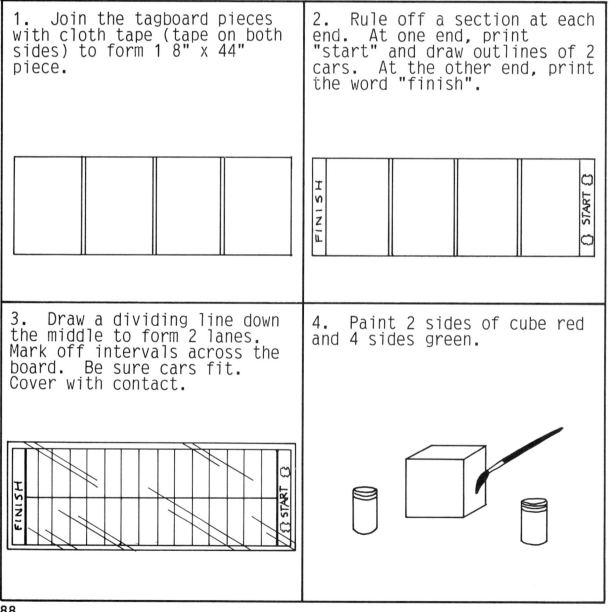

1.   Join the tagboard pieces with cloth tape (tape on both sides) to form 1 8" x 44" piece.

2.   Rule off a section at each end. At one end, print "start" and draw outlines of 2 cars. At the other end, print the word "finish".

3.   Draw a dividing line down the middle to form 2 lanes. Mark off intervals across the board. Be sure cars fit. Cover with contact.

4.   Paint 2 sides of cube red and 4 sides green.

Take-Apart People

HOW TO USE IT

Children take the dolls apart and put them together. Use as a weather doll or for a unit on clothing. Demonstrate inserting brass fasteners to attach head, arms and legs. (For very young children, use Velcro instead.) Call attention to the way feet and hands face when doll is assembled correctly. They will look funny reversed. Have children look at their own hands and feet and notice where their thumbs and toes point. Cut doll clothes out of tagboard, fabric, colored plastic or wallpaper samples. Punch holes in clothes to fit over brass fasteners so children can change outfits. Older children may want to cut out or make doll clothes.

WHAT IT DOES

Teaches recognition and awareness of body parts and their appropriate placement. Encourages language development through talking about ideas and words associated with self such as names of body parts, words for clothes, ways of moving the parts (i.e.: shaking head, waving arms, kicking feet). Encourages development of small motor coordination through putting together and taking apart dolls, dressing, moving and playing with them. Can make heads with different facial expressions and use to talk about feelings.

WHAT YOU NEED TO MAKE IT

patterns for arms, legs, body, head

tagboard

clear contact

hole punch

BRASS FASTENERS

5 brass fasteners

scissors*

markers

fabrics

pencil

shoe box to store

HOW TO MAKE IT

1. Trace patterns on tagboard for boy and girl dolls. Make extra heads to use for different expressions and cut out.

2. Draw features on face and make happy, sad or surprised expressions. Color dolls, if you wish.

3. Punch holes in body cut-outs as indicated on pattern and assemble doll with brass fasteners.

4. Cut out clothes for doll, making things for different seasons (i.e.: rain coat, snow suit, etc.).

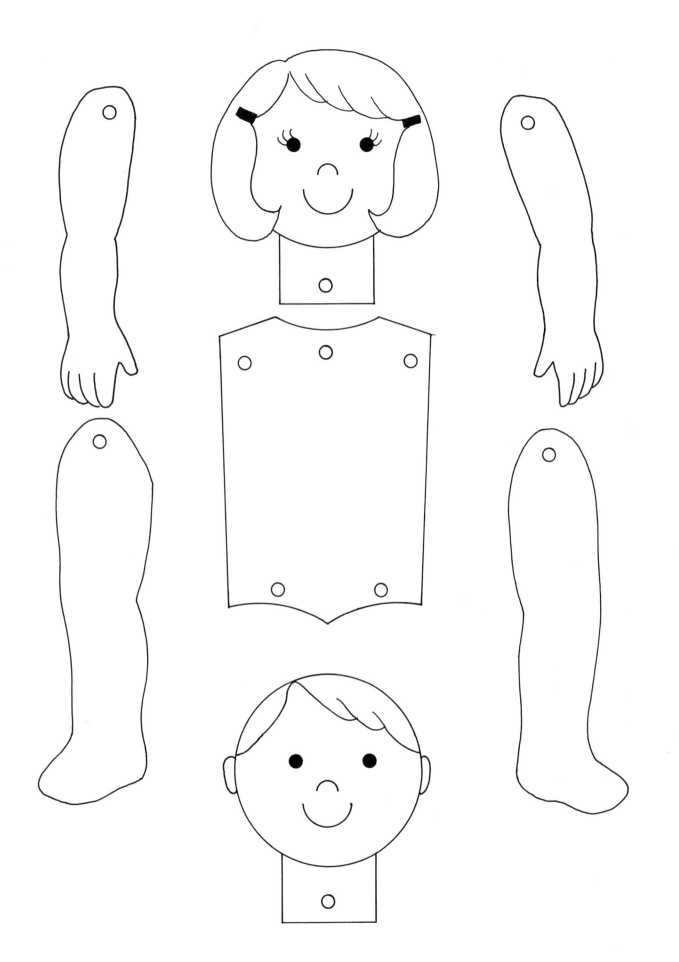

Tic-Tac-Toe

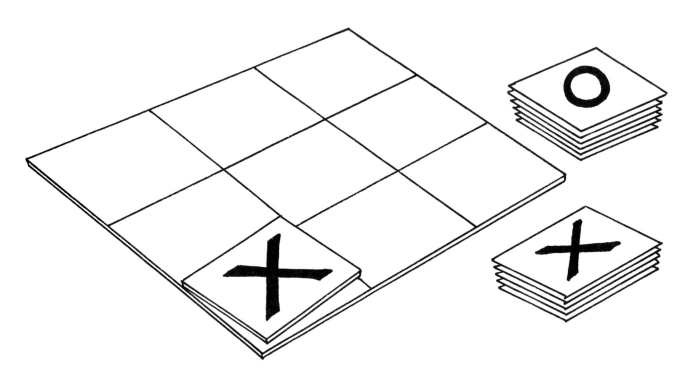

HOW TO USE IT

Can be played by two to four
children, ages 4 and up. If 4
children are playing, have an
X team and an O team. Divide
the X and O cards into
separate piles. Children take
turns placing X's and O's on
the board trying to get 3 of a
kind in a row, in as many rows
as they can. On a score pad,
keep track of how many rows
there are of 3 X's and 3 O's,
counting rows in all
directions. If there are no
rows of 3 X's or O's, give a
point to an animal (i. e.,
cat) drawn at the top of a
third column. Preschool
children will not try to
prevent each other from making
complete rows. School-agers
will develop strategies and be
more concerned about winning.

WHAT IT DOES

Helps develop many pre-math
and logical thinking skills,
including sequencing, sorting
same and different, counting,
etc. Illustrates the concept
of a "set", as 3 of the same
item (X or O) in a specific
order are required to score.
Older children may use it to
develop planning strategies in
playing a game.

WHAT YOU NEED TO MAKE IT

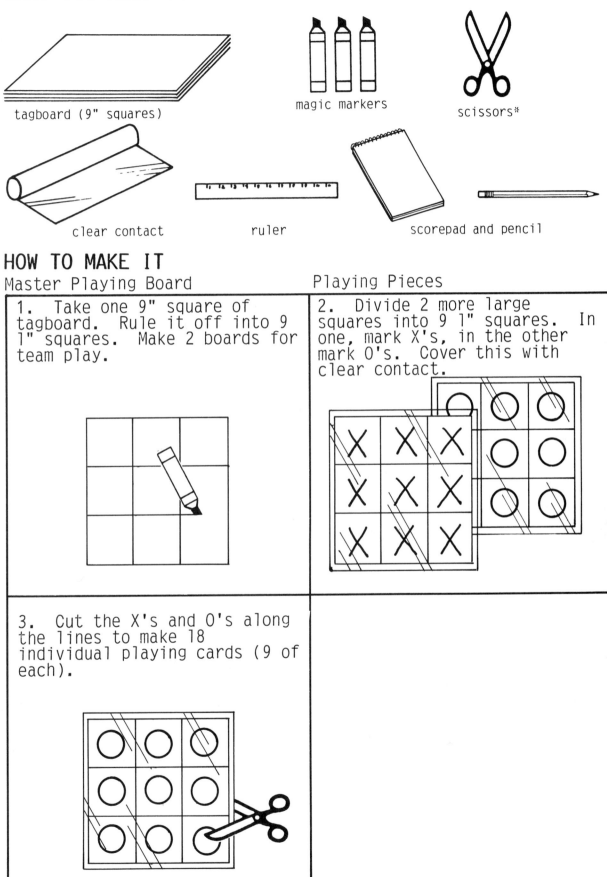

tagboard (9" squares)

magic markers

scissors*

clear contact

ruler

scorepad and pencil

HOW TO MAKE IT

Master Playing Board

Playing Pieces

1. Take one 9" square of tagboard. Rule it off into 9 1" squares. Make 2 boards for team play.

2. Divide 2 more large squares into 9 1" squares. In one, mark X's, in the other mark O's. Cover this with clear contact.

3. Cut the X's and O's along the lines to make 18 individual playing cards (9 of each).

What's My Number?

HOW TO USE IT

Children match the large plastic numeral to its outline on each master card. They can count out the correct number of objects indicated for each numeral and match to the dots indicated on each card. A variety of objects can be used for counters such as buttons, poker chips, etc. Use numbers 1 to 5 for younger children (3-4) and to 9 for older preschoolers (3 1/2-5).

Variation: Cards can be mounted on styrofoam. Pegs, golf tees or colored toothpicks can be used as counters, poking them in each slot.

WHAT IT DOES

Helps children recognize numerals and provides practice in matching them. Counting and matching objects individually helps children learn 1-to-1 number correspondence. Also provides exposure to the written word for each number.

WHAT YOU NEED TO MAKE IT

4 1 0 9

plastic numerals (used to hang on houses for address)

tagboard

objects (i.e., poker chips, buttons) for use as counters

clear contact

scissors*

markers

HOW TO MAKE IT

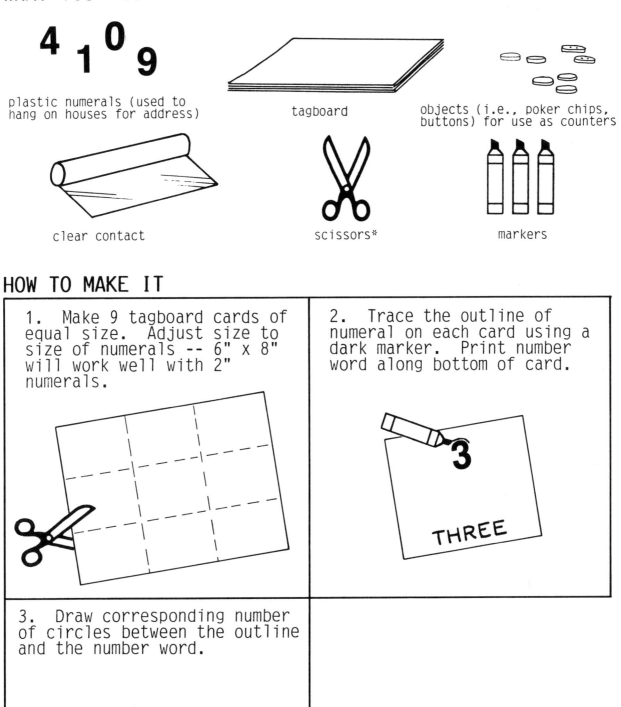

1. Make 9 tagboard cards of equal size. Adjust size to size of numerals -- 6" x 8" will work well with 2" numerals.

2. Trace the outline of numeral on each card using a dark marker. Print number word along bottom of card.

3. Draw corresponding number of circles between the outline and the number word.

Where's the Scoop?

HOW TO USE IT

Children match the semi-circular "scoops" to the "cone" of the same color. Encourage them to tell you what color they are matching and/or to point to or tell you other things that are the same color.

Variations: Can use as a number matching game by writing numbers on the cones with wipe-off crayons or washable markers and sticking 1 to 8 star stickers or small dots on 1 side of each "scoop". For easy number match keep the marker color consistent with the color match. For a more difficult game, vary it. Numbers will wipe off with a damp tissue or sponge.

WHAT IT DOES

Helps teach color matching and recognition for 2-3 year olds. Finding the scoops and putting them in the outline shape encourages eye-hand coordination.

Number match variation helps teach number recognition and awareness. In addition, extra "scoops" could be made to match quantity (i. e., putting 8 scoops on the #8 cone, etc.).

WHAT YOU NEED TO MAKE IT

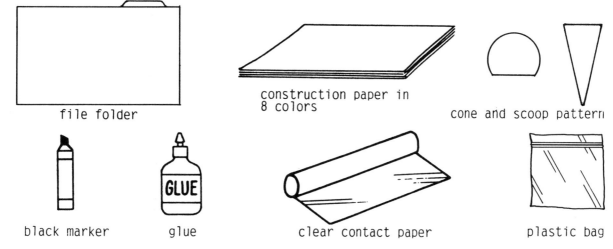

file folder

construction paper in 8 colors

cone and scoop pattern

black marker

glue

clear contact paper

plastic bag

HOW TO MAKE IT

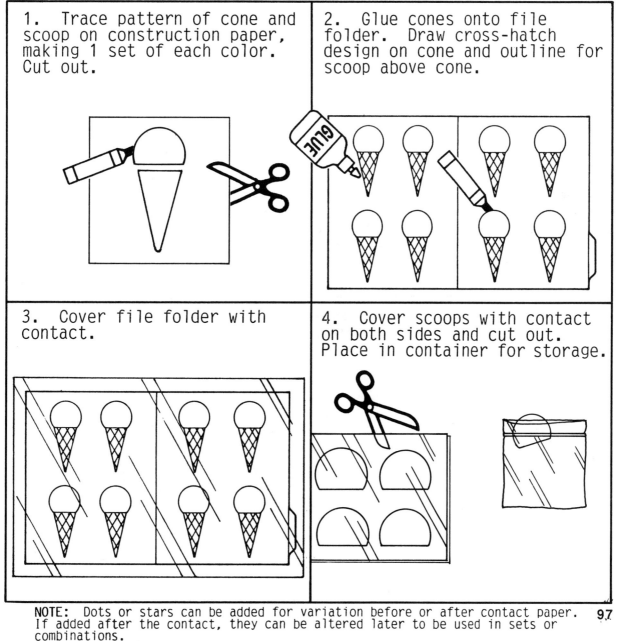

1. Trace pattern of cone and scoop on construction paper, making 1 set of each color. Cut out.

2. Glue cones onto file folder. Draw cross-hatch design on cone and outline for scoop above cone.

3. Cover file folder with contact.

4. Cover scoops with contact on both sides and cut out. Place in container for storage.

NOTE: Dots or stars can be added for variation before or after contact paper. If added after the contact, they can be altered later to be used in sets or combinations.

LIDS

Bottle Cap Counters

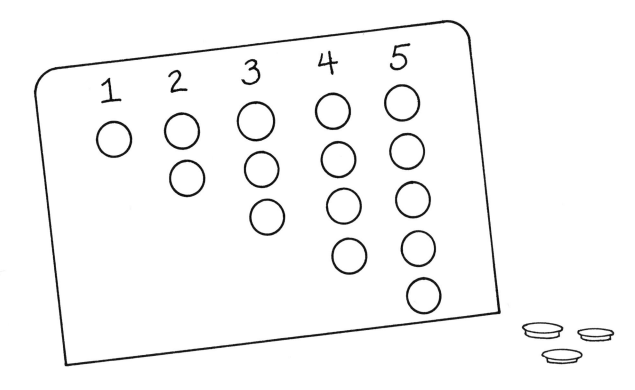

HOW TO USE IT

Use in a variety of matching games. For number matching game, child arranges bottle caps in rows counting out the appropriate number. Use numbers 1-5 for younger children, add 6 - 10 for older preschoolers. Can make a color matching game as well by writing each number in a different color. Children use caps of color indicated.

Variations: 1. Sort lids by colors into matching color bowls. 2. Attach number cards to bowls and have children count out that number for each bowl. 3. Concentration game. Mount small stickers (2 of each design) inside bottle caps. Place face down. Children take turns finding a match.

WHAT IT DOES

Helps children learn about numbers by actually counting out the correct amount for each number, reinforcing the concept of 1-to-1 number correspondence. Variations provide practice in learning to recognize and match colors and pictures of objects, which encourages visual-perceptual skill development. Provides a selection of activities adapted to differing ability levels. Simple number-color matching and sorting for younger children, concentration games for older ones.

WHAT YOU NEED TO MAKE IT

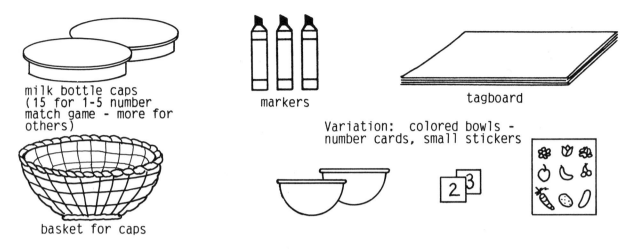

milk bottle caps
(15 for 1-5 number
match game - more for
others)

markers

tagboard

basket for caps

Variation: colored bowls -
number cards, small stickers

HOW TO MAKE IT

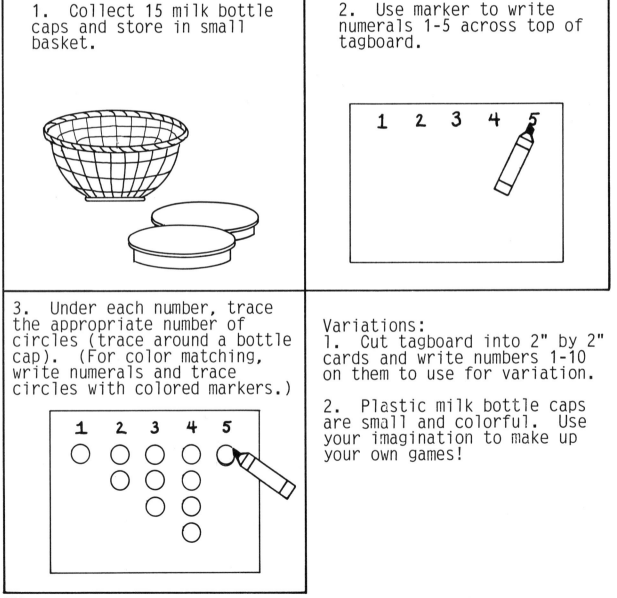

1. Collect 15 milk bottle caps and store in small basket.

2. Use marker to write numerals 1-5 across top of tagboard.

1   2   3   4   5

3. Under each number, trace the appropriate number of circles (trace around a bottle cap). (For color matching, write numerals and trace circles with colored markers.)

1   2   3   4   5

Variations:
1. Cut tagboard into 2" by 2" cards and write numbers 1-10 on them to use for variation.

2. Plastic milk bottle caps are small and colorful. Use your imagination to make up your own games!

Copycat Covers

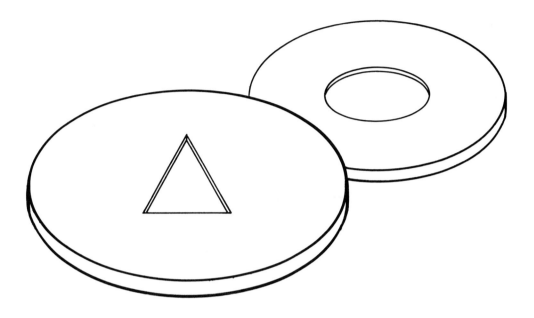

HOW TO USE IT

Children trace shapes or patterns on paper. Can be used singly or in combination to create design pictures. Children can color or decorate the shapes or designs in any way they wish. They can be used for patterns for spatter, roller or sponge painting. Ask children what objects the shapes could be and what could be added to them to make them look like that object (i. e.: squares to house or blocks, circles to faces, balls, etc.). Topical patterns such as pumpkins, hearts, holiday symbols, etc., can be used for special projects.

WHAT IT DOES

Tracing encourages the development of eye-hand coordination and small muscle control needed to follow the edge of any pattern and to manipulate crayons or pencils. Helps children learn shapes or pattern discrimination. Provides a starting point for child-created pictures using shapes or symbols in their design.

WHAT YOU NEED TO MAKE IT

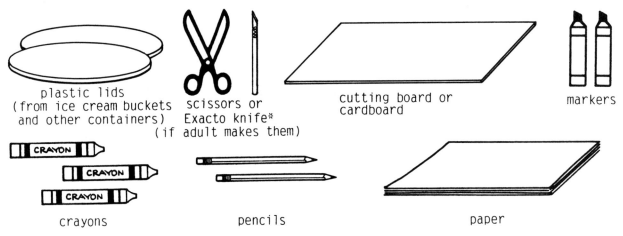

plastic lids
(from ice cream buckets
and other containers)

scissors or
Exacto knife*
(if adult makes them)

cutting board or
cardboard

markers

crayons

pencils

paper

HOW TO MAKE IT

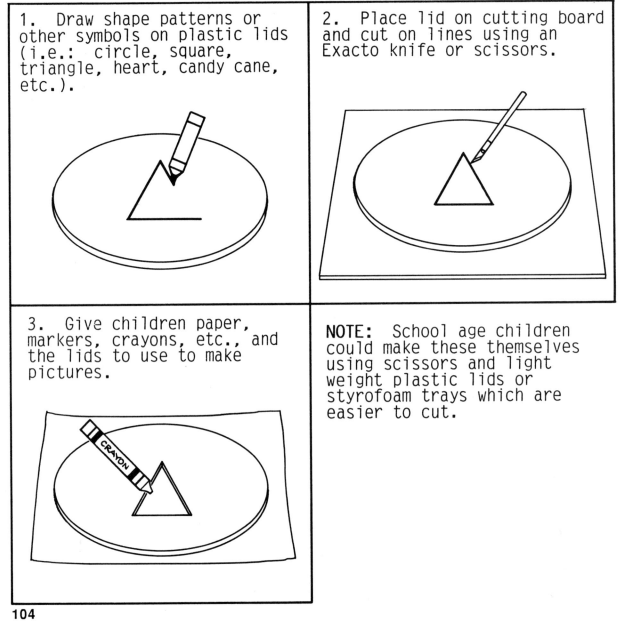

1. Draw shape patterns or other symbols on plastic lids (i.e.: circle, square, triangle, heart, candy cane, etc.).

2. Place lid on cutting board and cut on lines using an Exacto knife or scissors.

3. Give children paper, markers, crayons, etc., and the lids to use to make pictures.

NOTE: School age children could make these themselves using scissors and light weight plastic lids or styrofoam trays which are easier to cut.

Lid-der Box

HOW TO USE IT

Dump metal lids from can, replace plastic top and let the children drop the metal lids through the slot in the top into the coffee can one at a time. Infants and young toddlers love the noise the lids make. Make several can and lid sets to use with a small group of toddlers. Fabrics or pictures of single objects can be mounted inside the lids to increase interest. Toddlers can look for particular pictures or feel the various textures. Encourage older toddlers to find pictures or textures that are alike.

WHAT IT DOES

Provides practice in filling and dumping, a favorite activity of older infants and young toddlers because of their fascination with objects disappearing and reappearing. Helps in their experimenting with the concept of "object permanence" (learning that things exist when you can't see them). Also helps develop eye-hand coordination and provides sensory stimulation. Language development is encouraged by talking about the activity and naming the pictures.

WHAT YOU NEED TO MAKE IT

plastic lid from can

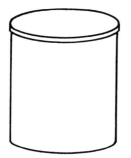

1 lb. coffee can**

contact paper

metal juice can lids**
(any size)

knife or
scissors*

GLUE

glue

small pictures or
fabric samples

HOW TO MAKE IT

1. Cut strip of contact paper to completely cover sides of coffee can.

2. Cut a slot about 1/2" wide and 2" to 3" long in plastic lid.

3. Make sure all lids (large and small) slide through easily and adjust slot size, if necessary.

4. Cut out simple pictures and/or samples of different fabric textures and glue on recessed side of metal lids.

**Check coffee can to be sure there are no sharp edges where the metal lid was removed. Use juice can lids that are smooth and removed by plastic pull strips, not can openers.

106

Lids Unlimited

HOW TO USE IT

The lids can be used for many different matching games. Begin by using the lids to talk about how they are alike and different. Select 2 lids that are exactly alike. Add a third that is different in some way and talk about how it is different (i.e.: begin with 2 small blue lids; add a large blue lid and discuss differences in size, or add a yellow lid and talk about color). Have children group the lids by a designated characteristic. Make cue cards; have children select one card and arrange lids accordingly. Also have children count the number of lids used.

WHAT IT DOES

Provides a lot of "homemade" learning opportunities for recognizing likenesses and differences, matching color, size, shape and categorizing. When used with cue cards, provides a logical thinking activity that also encourages pre-reading and pre-math skills. Variations encourage creativity by using lids in designs or pictures. Younger children may enjoy just manipulating lids, stacking them together, making towers or rows, or using them to fill and dump.

WHAT YOU NEED TO MAKE IT

plastic bottle tops

basket to hold lids

glue

tagboard   construction paper

clear contact

marker   scissors*   pencil   5" x 8" file cards

HOW TO MAKE IT

1. Collect large variety of bottle tops from all kinds of jars--spices, hair spray, soap, milk bottles, etc.

2. Trace lids on construction paper of a matching color. Cut out many of each size and color.

3. To make cue cards: Glue circles on file cards in a variety of combinations.

4. Place cue cards on tray with basket of lids.

VARIATIONS:

1. Sequencing Game: Arrange circles in rows of a patterned sequence by size or color or a combination of size and color. Make many different sequence arrangements. Children match the lids to the colored sequence on the card. Later have children match the same sequence off the card. Let them make up their own sequence patterns.

2. Puzzle or Picture Completion: Make some cue cards that are picture outlines and leave spaces for a lid or several lids to complete the picture.

Animals, birds, or insects work well, or pictures such as snowmen, gingerbread men, etc. Encourage children to notice and talk about what size will complete the picture. Give the children some blank paper and let them draw their own pictures to complete!

3. Design Cards: Make various free-form design cards using the circle cut-outs of all different colors and sizes. Children cover the circles with the lids to create 3-dimensional designs.

Scissors Holder

HOW TO USE IT

Use to store and carry scissors safely. Large coffee can holders can hold 10 or more scissors, small cans will hold 1 or 2 pair. Encourage children to return scissors to slots when not in use, placing point side down. For groups, use 2 medium-size cans so they can be spread out at a work table for easier use.

WHAT IT DOES

Provides a safe way for children to carry scissors and to keep them readily accessible for use. Encourages neatness since there is an individual slot for each scissors and children can easily take and replace them. Also protects the scissors from being dropped or falling off tables and shelves.

WHAT YOU NEED TO MAKE IT

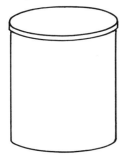

coffee or other
cans with
plastic lids

hand bottle can opener

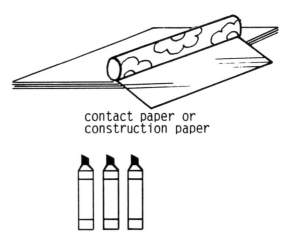

contact paper or
construction paper

scissors*

markers

HOW TO MAKE IT

1. Cover can with decorative contact paper or construction paper which the children can decorate.

2. Place plastic lid on can and poke evenly spaced holes around lid with the opener.

3. Put 1 pair of scissors into each hole--they will fit right in.

Tambourine

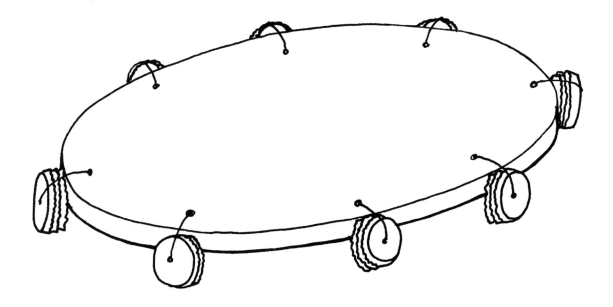

HOW TO USE IT

Children can use it alone as a tambourine to accompany records or as part of a group rhythm band. Encourage children to keep time to the music and shake the tambourine hard on the down beats and lighter on the upbeats. Also encourage them to keep time to the music (i.e.: shaking it fast or slow to match the rhythm of the music). Use with other homemade instruments in a music interest area. Encourage children to try different ways of using it, from shaking it to pounding it, and to notice differences in sounds.

WHAT IT DOES

Helps children recognize and follow rhythmic patterns and provides a way for them to be involved in creating music, making it more fun to learn. Instruments can serve as props for dramatic play or to accompany group singing. The tambourine is good to use as an introduction to percussion instruments.

WHAT YOU NEED TO MAKE IT

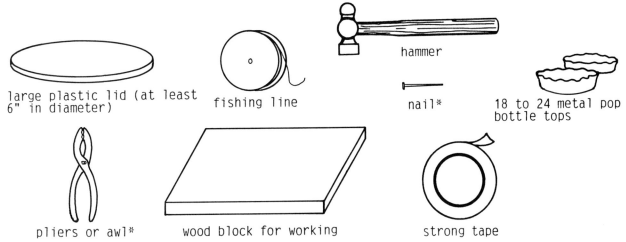

large plastic lid (at least 6" in diameter)

fishing line

hammer

nail*

18 to 24 metal pop bottle tops

pliers or awl*

wood block for working

strong tape

HOW TO MAKE IT

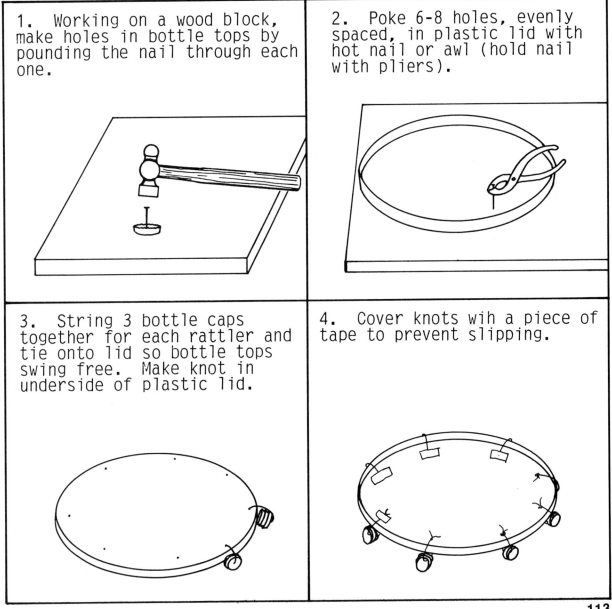

1. Working on a wood block, make holes in bottle tops by pounding the nail through each one.

2. Poke 6-8 holes, evenly spaced, in plastic lid with hot nail or awl (hold nail with pliers).

3. String 3 bottle caps together for each rattler and tie onto lid so bottle tops swing free. Make knot in underside of plastic lid.

4. Cover knots wih a piece of tape to prevent slipping.

MILK CARTONS

Chatter Cartons

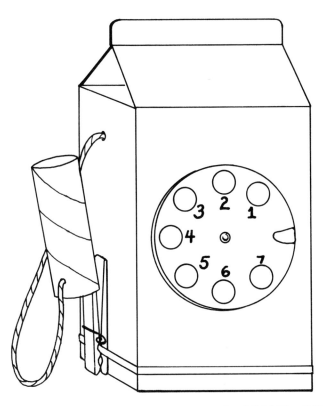

HOW TO USE IT

Encourage toddlers to use as a play telephone by pretending to talk or listen through the multi-purpose receiver "tube." Children also can manipulate the parts by turning the dial, or removing and replacing receiver on the clothespin hook. Toddlers may also use as a pull toy using the tube as a handle to take their phone with them.

WHAT IT DOES

Encourages talking even when the child is playing alone and beginning pretend play. A good toy to keep by a real phone to provide distraction when adult is on the phone. Manipulating parts develops eye-hand and small-motor coordination. Provides a safe toy the child can easily manipulate with readily replaceable parts. (Tube may disintegrate from wear so save some extras for a quick change as needed.)

WHAT YOU NEED TO MAKE IT

toilet paper tube

BRASS FASTENERS

1 1/2"-2" brass fastener

clip clothespin

large button

rubber band

thick yarn

1/2 gallon milk carton

heavy cardboard circle

contact paper (solid color)

marker

scissors*

masking tape

HOW TO MAKE IT

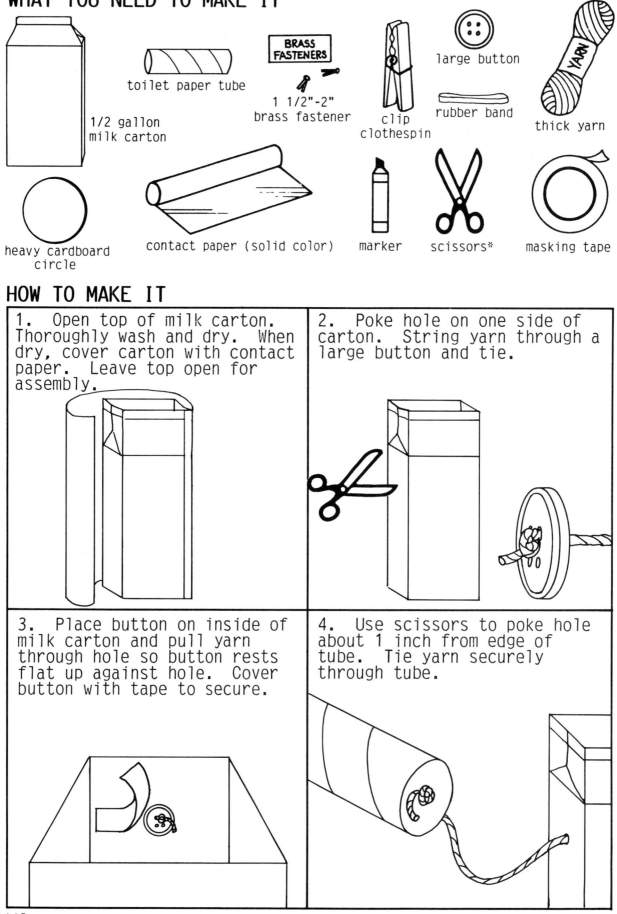

1. Open top of milk carton. Thoroughly wash and dry. When dry, cover carton with contact paper. Leave top open for assembly.

2. Poke hole on one side of carton. String yarn through a large button and tie.

3. Place button on inside of milk carton and pull yarn through hole so button rests flat up against hole. Cover button with tape to secure.

4. Use scissors to poke hole about 1 inch from edge of tube. Tie yarn securely through tube.

5. Cut a 3 1/2" circle from cardboard. Using scissors, poke holes (3/8" in diameter) in the dial. Add numerals. Poke 1 hole in center.

6. Poke a hole in front of milk carton, slightly above middle. Attach dial to milk carton with brass fastener.

7. Close milk carton with tape and cover top section with contact.

8. On receiver side, open clothespin and slip rubber band into hole; snap shut. Stretch rubber band around base of carton.

9. Place receiver on hook. If desired, draw dark circles around numbers, fastener and holes on cardboard circle to look like real dial.

Milk Carton Puppets

HOW TO USE IT

A variety of animals can be made to use in telling familiar stories and nursery rhymes. Bears, bunnies, kittens, puppies and lambs are particularly useful. Smaller size milk cartons (pints) can be used by the children to make puppets that look like animals or people (soldiers, firefighters, etc.) for stories or as props in dramatic play.

WHAT IT DOES

Puppets encourage children to tell stories, developing language and memory skills. Often children who are shy about talking or seem to forget what they want to say are more comfortable playing a puppet role. Puppets also encourage children to create original stories. All of these are skills that contribute to reading readiness and literacy.

WHAT YOU NEED TO MAKE IT

toilet paper roll

glue

scissors*

staples*

1/2 gallon cardboard milk cartons

needle, thread

appropriate fur fabric and felt for animals being constructed

HOW TO MAKE IT

1. Cut off top section of milk carton (the part opened for pouring). Wash and dry thoroughly.

2. Place milk carton on its bottom. Mark a line 3" down from the top rim. On both sides, draw an arched line from dot to bottom corners. Cut along the line.

3"

3. Turn carton so bottom is up. Cut a square of felt (the color you want for the mouth) the size of the milk carton bottom. Glue it on.

4. Flip open the 1/2 of the carton you have cut. The bottom becomes the mouth and the smaller, arched section becomes the puppet's face.

5. Cut fur to cover the milk carton and attach with staples.

6. Sew small pieces of fur to form arms and sew or staple to main puppet.

7. Cut ears from cardboard tube. Cut felt for inner ear and fur for outer section. Staple ears to head. Glue or staple fur, then felt, to ears.

8. Cut black and other felt pieces for eyes, nose and decorations for puppet. Glue on facial features and decorations.

9. Practice folding puppet's mouth a few times by inserting hand into elongated milk carton.

PAPER BAGS/
PLASTIC BAGS

Cue Me In

HOW TO USE IT

Give each child a medium-size paper bag with a cue card in it. Children then walk around the room or yard to collect in their bags items that match the cue cards. Samples of cue card items and their use are:
● A colored strip of paper; children find things of the same color
● A "shape" card; children find items that are that shape
● A card with a numeral (4) and/or the same number of dots (. . . .) on it; children collect four items

Vary the cue cards in each child's bag so they are all looking for different color items, etc. As the children get used to this game (or for the older children), the cue cards can combine tasks (i.e.: shape and numbers).

WHAT IT DOES

Can be used to teach color, shape and number recognition. Teaches children to look for and match items, to think about categories of things and to make judgments in solving problems (i.e., finding things). Good to stimulate discussion of all of the above as you talk about and compare what the children found and collected. Encourages them to notice specific character-istics or details of items in the environment. Practice in a pre-reading skill; the child is reading the signs on the cue card and following directions.

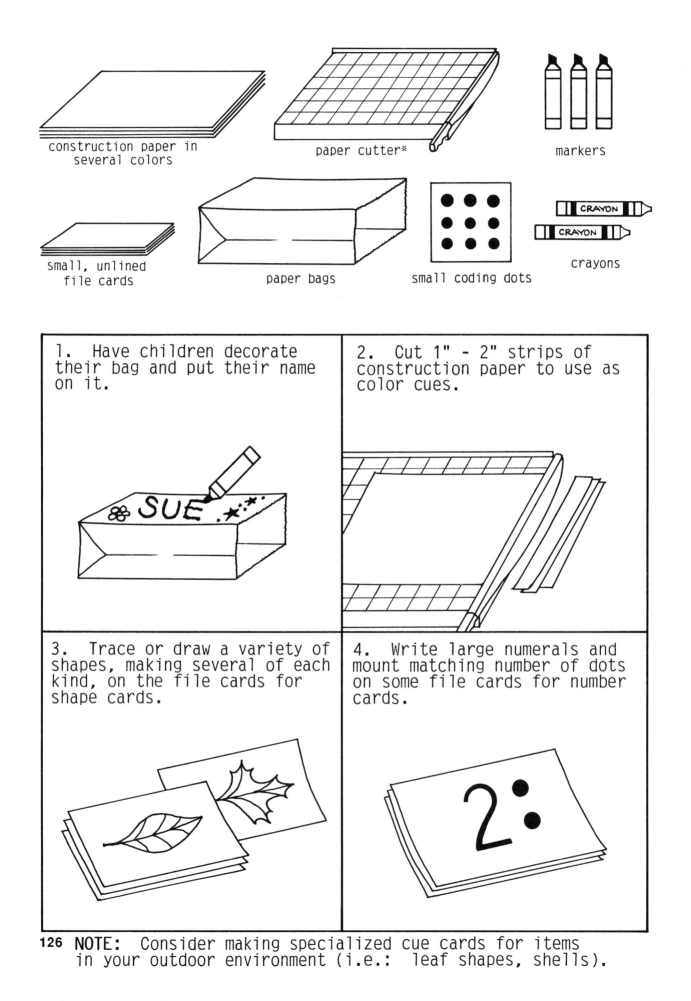

construction paper in several colors

paper cutter*

markers

small, unlined file cards

paper bags

small coding dots

crayons

1. Have children decorate their bag and put their name on it.

SUE

2. Cut 1" - 2" strips of construction paper to use as color cues.

3. Trace or draw a variety of shapes, making several of each kind, on the file cards for shape cards.

4. Write large numerals and mount matching number of dots on some file cards for number cards.

2

NOTE: Consider making specialized cue cards for items in your outdoor environment (i.e.: leaf shapes, shells).

Fancy Fish

HOW TO USE IT

Children use markers to color the fish-shaped bags. Before making, show children pictures of fish and discuss where they live and what they look like. Call attention to bright colors, tail shapes, eye placement, etc. For toddlers and 3-year-olds, prepare fish shapes in advance. Older children can create their own with help in tying. Fish can be used for room decorations, as a tropical fish display or in dramatic play about fishing, snorkeling or scuba diving. Paper clips can be put on the fish and children can "fish" for them with magnets tied on homemade fishing poles.

WHAT IT DOES

A fun craft activity that can help teach about tropical fish or ocean life. Illustrates shape and characteristics of fish. Use to create an interesting table display about the ocean with addition of other items such as shells, coral, rocks, etc. Creating the fish uses fine-motor skills. The use of fish in pretend play or display encourages development of language and imagination. Make lots of fish and let children think of fun things to do with them.

WHAT YOU NEED TO MAKE IT

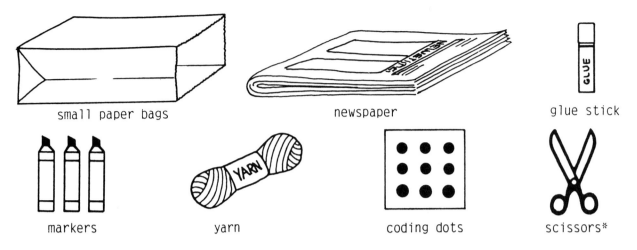

small paper bags   newspaper   glue stick

markers   yarn   coding dots   scissors*

HOW TO MAKE IT

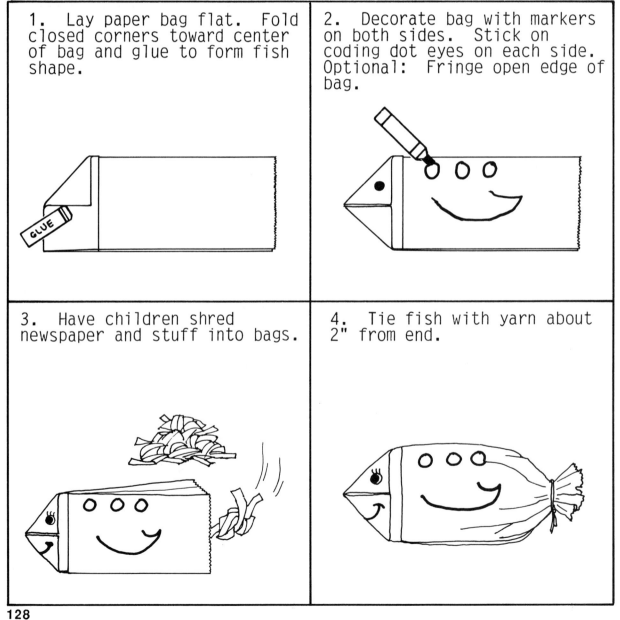

1. Lay paper bag flat. Fold closed corners toward center of bag and glue to form fish shape.

2. Decorate bag with markers on both sides. Stick on coding dot eyes on each side. Optional: Fringe open edge of bag.

3. Have children shred newspaper and stuff into bags.

4. Tie fish with yarn about 2" from end.

Paperbag Kickball

HOW TO USE IT

Use outdoors or in a large indoor area. Have each child make his/her own ball to practice kicking and throwing skills. In pairs, have children kick or throw balls back and forth. To encourage cooperative play, devise simple team games, using walls or trees as "goals". Establish an obstacle course and kick balls around it.

Variations: For toddlers - Tie a string to it and let them use it as a pull toy. Hang from a branch or door jamb and let children practice batting at it with their hands or lightweight paddles.

WHAT IT DOES

Provides an easy object for practicing kicking, throwing or batting. Encourages large motor coordination, eye-hand and eye-foot coordination. Provides a simple means for encouraging cooperation without competition, since you can make enough for everyone to have their own.

Very young children love tearing up the newspapers to make these (also an eye-hand coordination task).

The process teaches how to make an object to use in play.

WHAT YOU NEED TO MAKE IT

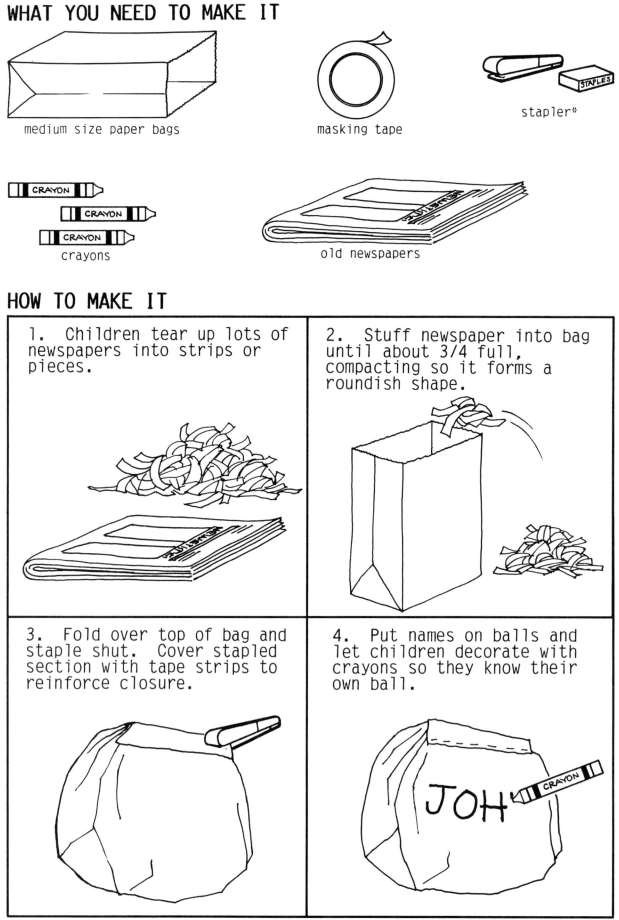

medium size paper bags

masking tape

stapler*

crayons

old newspapers

HOW TO MAKE IT

1. Children tear up lots of newspapers into strips or pieces.

2. Stuff newspaper into bag until about 3/4 full, compacting so it forms a roundish shape.

3. Fold over top of bag and staple shut. Cover stapled section with tape strips to reinforce closure.

4. Put names on balls and let children decorate with crayons so they know their own ball.

JOH

Simple Puzzle Repair

HOW TO USE IT

Use this technique to encourage children to care for and repair materials. Demonstrate the process of mixing the wood putty, lining the empty puzzle space with plastic wrap and filling it in with wood putty. Discuss what can be done when the piece dries -- sanding edges and painting or coloring the piece to match the puzzle. Use in a dramatic play fix-it shop. School-age children will be able to do this on their own after some demonstration and with some supervision. Younger children can assist in phases of the process such as sanding and painting.

WHAT IT DOES

Helps save money by providing a way to extend usefulness of puzzles after a piece has been lost. Teaches about care, maintenance and repair of materials and facilitates a discussion about when something can be repaired (too many lost pieces won't work). Encourages development of home fix-it skills as well as feelings of accomplishment in a "real" work task. Encourages planning, following directions, and problem-solving (how to make the piece look right for the puzzle).

WHAT YOU NEED TO MAKE IT

puzzles with missing piece

wood putty

plastic wrap

acrylic paints

small paint brushes

sandpaper

spoon

HOW TO MAKE IT

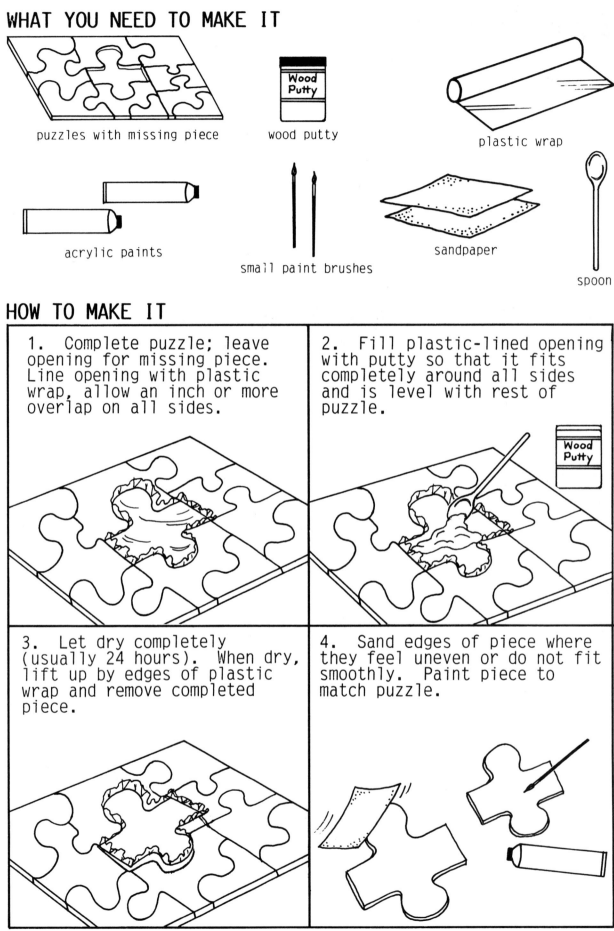

1. Complete puzzle; leave opening for missing piece. Line opening with plastic wrap, allow an inch or more overlap on all sides.

2. Fill plastic-lined opening with putty so that it fits completely around all sides and is level with rest of puzzle.

Wood Putty

3. Let dry completely (usually 24 hours). When dry, lift up by edges of plastic wrap and remove completed piece.

4. Sand edges of piece where they feel uneven or do not fit smoothly. Paint piece to match puzzle.

Squish Bags

HOW TO USE IT

Let the children squeeze and manipulate the bag to feel the texture and blend the colors together. Can add additional food coloring to darken or change color. Use as long as the children are interested in manipulating it. The colored shaving cream can later be dumped onto a piece of paper or a cookie sheet to be used for fingerpainting or children can pretend to fingerpaint on the bag with the colored shaving cream inside.

WHAT IT DOES

Provides a fun, sensory exploration. Toddlers really love squeezing these bags, although pre-schoolers also enjoy it.

A very good manipulative activity that also teaches the children to observe how colors can be mixed together to create different colors. Be sure to talk about what the children are doing and what is happening as they squeeze the bags. Can also provide a non-messy introduction to finger painting for children who are reluctant to try the real thing.

WHAT YOU NEED TO MAKE IT

shaving cream   food coloring   small or medium size
Ziploc bags

HOW TO MAKE IT

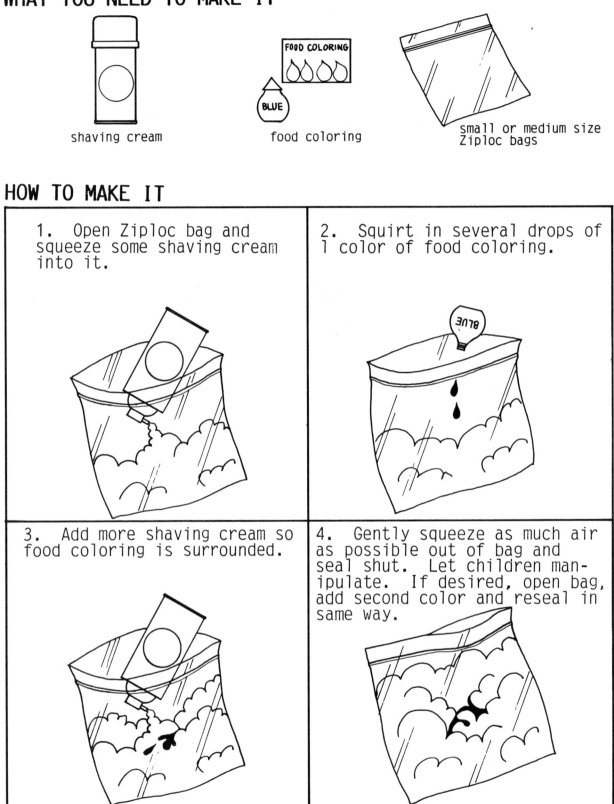

1. Open Ziploc bag and squeeze some shaving cream into it.

2. Squirt in several drops of 1 color of food coloring.

3. Add more shaving cream so food coloring is surrounded.

4. Gently squeeze as much air as possible out of bag and seal shut. Let children manipulate. If desired, open bag, add second color and reseal in same way.

HINT: Use sandwich size bags for manipulation and color mixing. Use the larger size bag if you wish to use them for fingerpainting as well.

Ziploc Dot-to-Dot

HOW TO USE IT

Select a variety of tracing or dot-to-dot pictures and show the children how to insert one picture into the plastic bag. Children trace the picture or complete the dot-to-dot using washable markers or erasable wax crayons. When completed, child can use a damp sponge or washcloth to wipe off the picture and do it over again or turn over and do the picture on the other side. Ask children if they can guess the picture in dot-to-dots as they work.

Variation: Make pattern cards of children's names, insert in bag and let them practice tracing their name.

WHAT IT DOES

Provides a method to prolong the life of dot-to-dot or tracing pages from coloring books so that children can use them more than once.

Tracing encourages development of fine motor skills and eye-hand coordination. Working with numbered dot-to-dots helps children learn about number sequence, following directions and using clues to find an answer. Tracing letters and printing names helps children get ready for writing and builds self-esteem.

WHAT YOU NEED TO MAKE IT

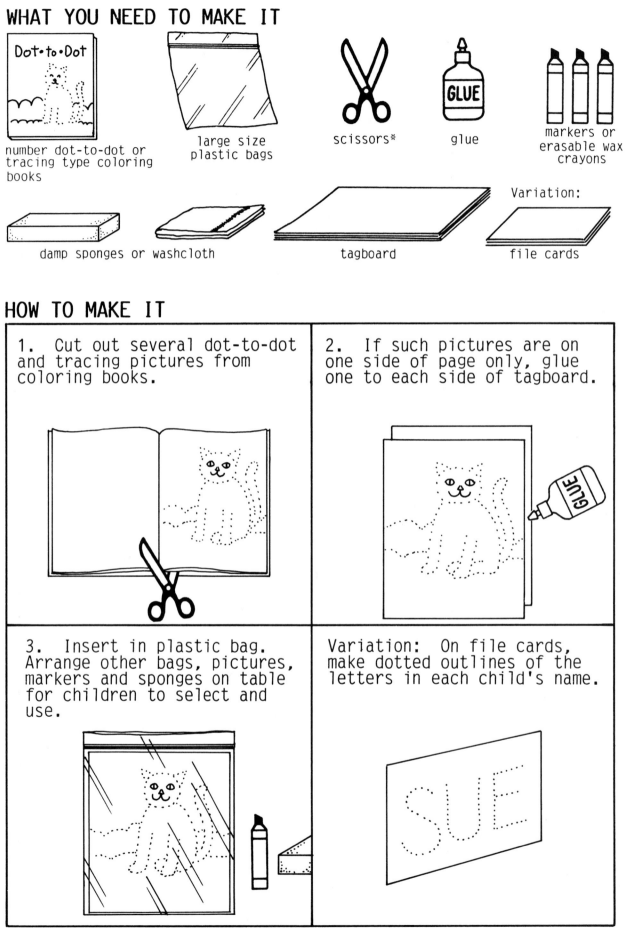

number dot-to-dot or tracing type coloring books

large size plastic bags

scissors*

glue

markers or erasable wax crayons

damp sponges or washcloth

tagboard

Variation:

file cards

HOW TO MAKE IT

1. Cut out several dot-to-dot and tracing pictures from coloring books.

2. If such pictures are on one side of page only, glue one to each side of tagboard.

3. Insert in plastic bag. Arrange other bags, pictures, markers and sponges on table for children to select and use.

Variation: On file cards, make dotted outlines of the letters in each child's name.

136

PLASTIC CONTAINERS

Bucket Brigade

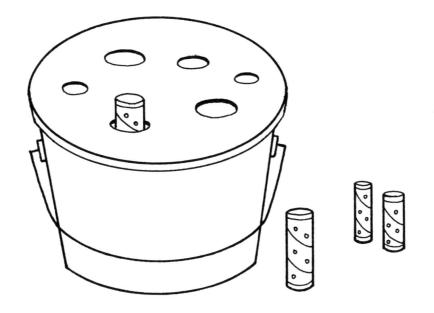

HOW TO USE IT

Children dump the curlers and try to fit them through the holes into the bucket. The small curlers fit through any hole, but the large ones require some searching for a larger opening that will work. Adult will need to assist in replacing the lid. Repeat the "dump-and-fill" process as long as toddler remains interested, providing assistance as needed. Toddlers also enjoy just carrying the bucket around. Talk with the toddlers about what they are doing as well as the sizes and colors of the curlers.

WHAT IT DOES

Provides a very portable and enjoyable fill-and-dump toy for toddlers and older infants. Encourages eye-hand coordination, small-muscle development and thinking and problem-solving skills. Young toddlers are fascinated with fill-and-dump toys because of their need to explore and to try to understand the idea of things existing when they can't see them. With adult guidance, the disappearance and reappearance of the curlers can encourage language development, reasoning, and making associations.

WHAT YOU NEED TO MAKE IT

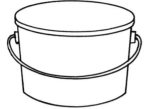

large plastic bucket with lid (ice cream or soap)

plastic curlers (assorted sizes)

Exacto knife or scissors*

markers

HOW TO MAKE IT

1. Remove lid from bucket. On lid, trace around each size curler, making 2 of each.

2. Cut out holes with knife or scissors. Put curlers in bucket and replace lid.

Hanging Planter

HOW TO USE IT

Have children assist in
filling the planter with dirt,
planting the plants and caring
for them. Also can make
individual planters from
smaller-size plastic pop
bottles. School-age children
can make braided yarn tails to
hold the planter.

WHAT IT DOES

Makes an attractive planter.
Can be added to a science area
to help teach about the care
of plants. Small planters
would make a very nice
Mother's Day gift.

WHAT YOU NEED TO MAKE IT

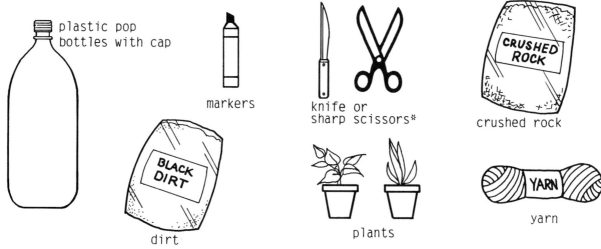

plastic pop
bottles with cap

markers

knife or
sharp scissors*

crushed rock

BLACK
DIRT

dirt

plants

YARN

yarn

HOW TO MAKE IT

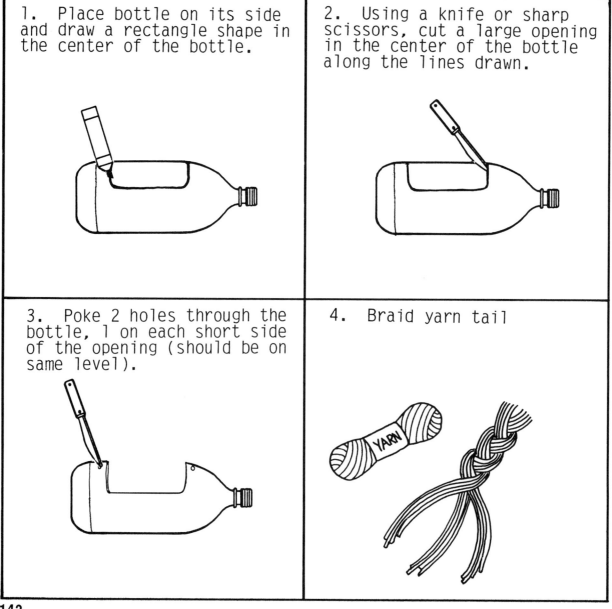

1. Place bottle on its side and draw a rectangle shape in the center of the bottle.

2. Using a knife or sharp scissors, cut a large opening in the center of the bottle along the lines drawn.

3. Poke 2 holes through the bottle, 1 on each short side of the opening (should be on same level).

4. Braid yarn tail

5. Thread yarn through holes. Tie large knot on inside to secure hanger.

6. Fill bottom of planter with crushed rock for drainage. Add dirt and plants.

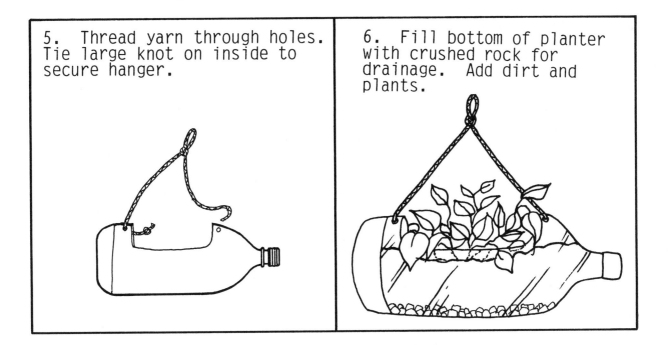

Ice Cream Bucket Chair

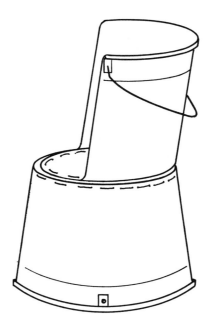

HOW TO USE IT

Use as a sturdy chair and extra storage unit for toddlers. Can be used in play areas or as a way for toddlers to have their own special chair and space. Let toddlers decorate their chairs with stickers and put their names on them. Can also be used by toddlers for storing their blanket or special cuddly toy. When needed, they can go find their comfort toy and special chair to get away from it all! Toddlers enjoy carrying their chair from place to place.

WHAT IT DOES

Provides a lightweight, easy-to-carry, toddler-size chair. Helps toddler have his/her own space. Provides for the development of self-esteem through recognition of individual possessions, furnishing an independent means of meeting needs for comfort and separateness during the day, and supplying a piece of "furniture" the child can handle alone. Provides a means of some physical separation and extra storage of special treasures.

WHAT YOU NEED TO MAKE IT

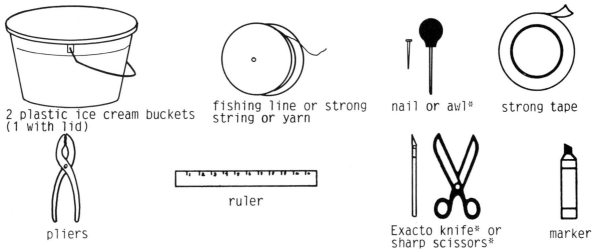

2 plastic ice cream buckets
(1 with lid)

fishing line or strong
string or yarn

nail or awl*

strong tape

pliers

ruler

Exacto knife* or
sharp scissors*

marker

HOW TO MAKE IT

1. Remove lids. On one bucket draw a slight diagonal line from top to bottom as shown in drawing.

2. Cut along that line. Round off bottom of bucket.

3. Place the cut bucket on top of the other one, bottoms together. Bottom of upper bucket will be about an inch smaller at one end.

4. Heat nail or awl. (Hold hot nail with pliers.) Poke holes through both layers, about 5/8" from the edge and about 1" apart. Be sure holes line up.

5. On lower bucket, make a set of holes around the side of the bucket 1/2" down and 1" apart. These should line up with holes made in step 4.

6. Lace seats together with fishing line by going through both seat layers until two pieces are securely attached. Tie off inside the bucket.

7. Replace lid on lower bucket for stability and remove handle by twisting it out. Handle remains on the upper bucket for carrying.

8. Cover cut plastic edges on upper part of chair with tape.

Magnet Mysteries

HOW TO USE IT

After initial demonstration, children bury or hide the metal objects in the sand and then use the magnet to seek them out. The magnets should not have to touch the sand, but should be strong enough to pull the objects out of the sand. Strong bar, horseshoe or "cow" magnets will work. Children can count the items they put in the sand and count to see if they have them all when finished. Store metal items in plastic bowl when not in use. The container and magnets can be kept in the sand bucket (with lid on) for storage. Best if used by 1 or 2 children at a time.

WHAT IT DOES

Provides a fun activity that allows children to experiment with magnets. Poking and hiding the objects provides sensory stimulation. Counting and remembering if all items are recovered provides practice for cognitive and memory skills. Burying objects and removing them from the magnet provides practice in fine motor skills and grasping. Experimenting, observing, questioning and discussing results introduces children to the scientific method of inquiry.

Variation: Include some items the magnet will not pick up and talk about why.

WHAT YOU NEED TO MAKE IT

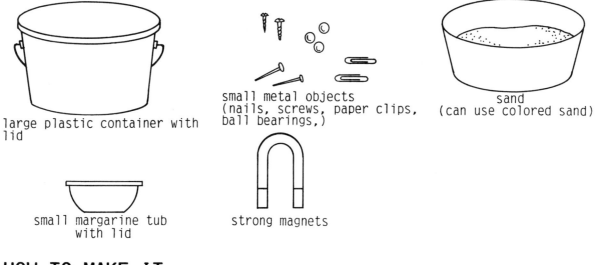

large plastic container with lid

small metal objects
(nails, screws, paper clips,
ball bearings,)

sand
(can use colored sand)

small margarine tub
with lid

strong magnets

HOW TO MAKE IT

1. Clean out container and let dry. Pour sand into container so it is 1/2 to 2/3 full. Cover with lid to store.

2. Collect the metal objects. Place in margarine tubs for storage.

Slow Motion Ocean

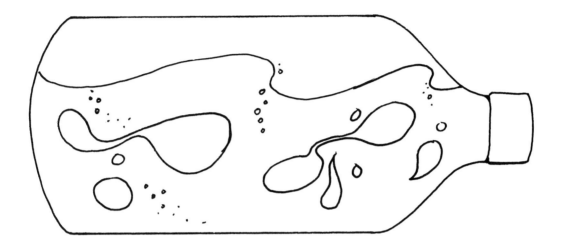

HOW TO USE IT

Holding the bottle upright, point out the two different sections made by water and oil.   Demonstrate wave action by tilting bottle slightly and slowly continue to move it up and down in the tilted position. After the demonstration, place in an area where children can practice using it themselves. Remind them that it has to be moved slowly for best effect. Discuss what is happening and what this looks like and why. Talk about "weight" of water and oil. Add objects to float in bottle and observe the effect. Make additional "oceans" by using different amounts of water and oil, or different size bottles. Write a story about your observations.

WHAT IT DOES

Illustrates wave action and the effect of water and oil on each other. (They don't mix!) Wave action is produced by water and oil continually trying to separate while the slow motion of the bottle keeps causing them to bump into each other. Good for teaching movement control. Shows position of heavier and lighter elements. Encourages experimentation, observation and testing of ideas (the scientific method). Fun to use in a seascape display or ocean interest area.

Variation: Make a smaller version with floating objects (tiny plastic fish, etc.) inside to use as an infant or bath toy.

WHAT YOU NEED TO MAKE IT

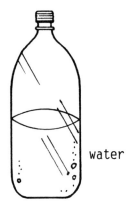
water

clear plastic pop
bottle with cap

FOOD COLORING

BLUE

blue or green food coloring

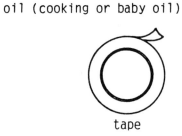
OIL

oil (cooking or baby oil)

GLUE

glue

tape

HOW TO MAKE IT

1. Thoroughly wash bottle. Fill half full with water.

2. Add a few drops of blue or green food coloring, shake to mix color.

BLUE

3. Add oil until bottle is 3/4 full.

OIL

4. Seal bottle tightly by gluing on the cap or taping it shut.

GLUE

NOTE: The more transluscent the bottle, the better it will be. Glass also works well but is heavier and could break in use.

Soap Bottle Pull Toy

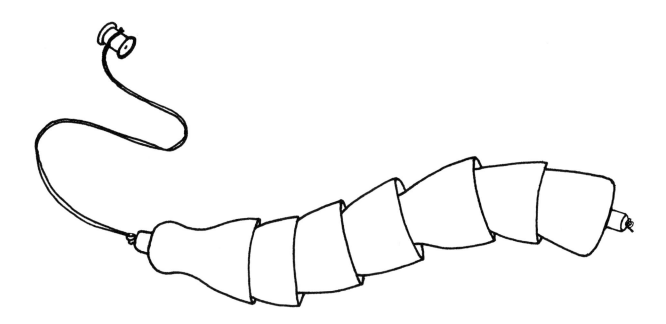

HOW TO USE IT

Toddlers enjoy pulling these around, experimenting with fast and slow and side-to-side movement. Adults can help them observe and learn to control the objects. Encourage the toddlers to pretend they are pulling trains or trucks and imitate the appropriate noises. Pull toy can also be used in a water table or bath to observe effect of movement through water. Be sure to talk about what the toddlers are doing and provide enough so each toddler can have his/her own. It is also a simple toy to make as a gift.

WHAT IT DOES

Encourages toddlers in imitative, parallel play. Pushing and pulling objects contributes not only to motor development, but also provides a feeling of control over an object, a key developmental need of toddlers. Imagination and language development are encouraged through discussion of concepts, ideas and sounds related to their play (i.e.: fast, slow, push, pull, train, choo-choo).

WHAT YOU NEED TO MAKE IT

 2 bottle caps

scissors or nail*

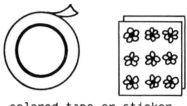

3'-4' string

plastic soap bottles

large spool

contact paper (optional)

colored tape or sticker
decorations (optional)

HOW TO MAKE IT

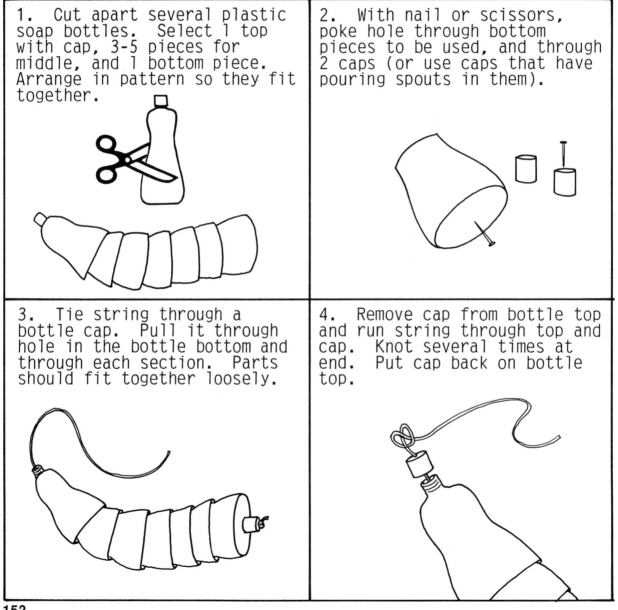

1. Cut apart several plastic soap bottles. Select 1 top with cap, 3-5 pieces for middle, and 1 bottom piece. Arrange in pattern so they fit together.

2. With nail or scissors, poke hole through bottom pieces to be used, and through 2 caps (or use caps that have pouring spouts in them).

3. Tie string through a bottle cap. Pull it through hole in the bottle bottom and through each section. Parts should fit together loosely.

4. Remove cap from bottle top and run string through top and cap. Knot several times at end. Put cap back on bottle top.

152

5. Leave about 18" of string. Loop through and tie around large spool to form handle.

6. Optional: decorate bottles with tape, contact paper, pictures or stickers.

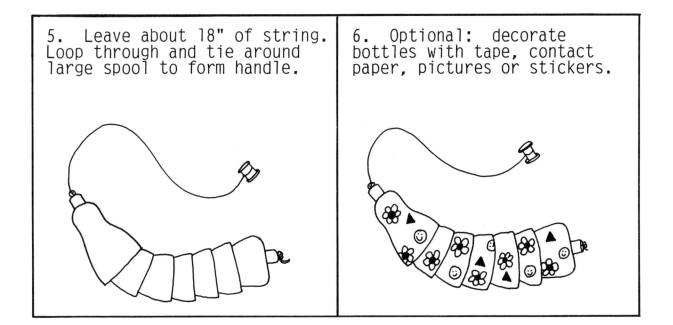

Soda Pop Drop

HOW TO USE IT

Can be used by all ages in different ways. For toddlers, demonstrate standing above bottle and dropping rings over bottle neck. As skill develops, encourage children to move farther away from the bottle. Give 2 children 2 or 3 rings and encourage them to take turns dropping them over the bottle. Talk about and count the rings that landed on the bottle and those that landed on the floor. Older preschoolers and school-agers could use this as a variation of a ring toss or horseshoe game. Taped circles can be made at intervals on the floor around the bottle and points assigned to where the ring lands. School-agers can form teams and keep track of scores, and make up rules for the game.

WHAT IT DOES

Teaches eye-hand coordination and provides practice in judging distance, position and direction, all useful perceptual motor skills. Introduces the idea of taking turns and playing simple games. Can provide practice in counting and simple-score keeping. For school-agers, can introduce the idea of teams, designing and organizing a court and deciding rules.

This game can be used both indoors and outside, and is easily adapted to each child's skill level.

WHAT YOU NEED TO MAKE IT

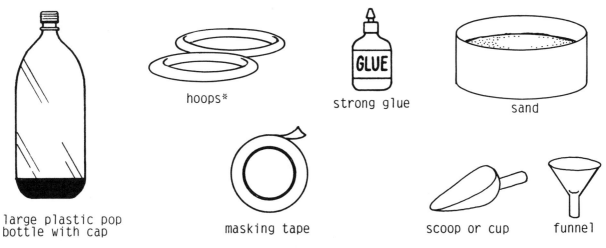

large plastic pop
bottle with cap

hoops*

strong glue

sand

masking tape

scoop or cup

funnel

HOW TO MAKE IT

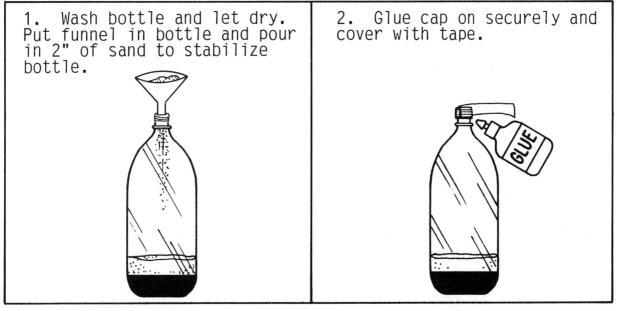

1. Wash bottle and let dry. Put funnel in bottle and pour in 2" of sand to stabilize bottle.

2. Glue cap on securely and cover with tape.

*A number of different items can be used for the hoops. Canning jar rings, plastic bracelets, large drapery rings, and large masking tape rolls will all work.

Twist & Turn

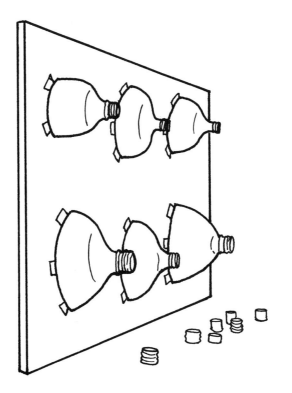

HOW TO USE IT

Children unscrew tops, remove and mix them up; then find the ones that fit and screw them back together again. Can be used by one child as an individual activity or two children could work together taking turns picking a top and trying to find the correct match. Provide a small container to keep tops in when they are unattached to bottles so they don't get lost.

WHAT IT DOES

Provides practice in eye-hand coordination, visual discrimination and fine motor skills used to screw and unscrew the caps. Helps establish the association of 1 top of each bottle and encourages association of size match of top and bottle. Two-and-a-half to three-year-olds are fascinated by this activity.

WHAT YOU NEED TO MAKE IT

6 or 8 mixed size plastic
bottles with caps

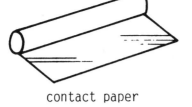

contact paper

heavy duty stapler

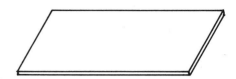

heavy cardboard or plywood

scissors*

felt (optional)

HOW TO MAKE IT

1. Cut off top section of 6 or 8 bottles at the shoulder, leaving 6 tabs on bottle.

2. Attach cut off bottle tops to board by stapling at tabs. Press flat against cardboard to staple.

3. Cover board with contact. Cut out circles to go around each bottle; be sure stapled sections are covered.

NOTES: 1. Be sure each cap fits only one bottle. Check each one before making game. 2. If desired, cover back of board with felt.

STICKERS

Clock Matching

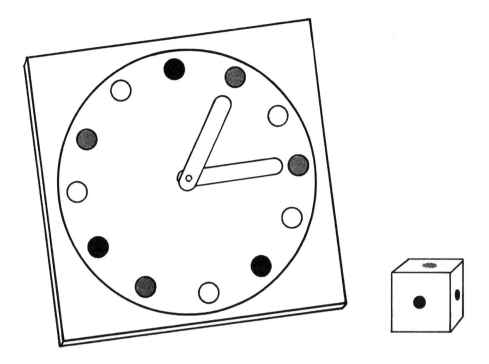

HOW TO USE IT

The clock face can be used by 1 or 2 children to find the matching shapes, colors or pictures. One child points 1 hand to a picture or color, the second child moves the other hand to the picture or color that matches. The activity can be varied by using accompanying dice. To use with 1 die: Child rolls die, then moves hands to matching pictures. To use with 2 dice: Child rolls dice, moves 1 hand to match picture on one die and moves the second hand to match the other picture. Children take turns rolling dice and finding pictures.

WHAT IT DOES

Teaches recognition of likenesses and differences and, depending on the pictures used on the face boards and dice, teaches color, letter or shape recognition. Encourages 2 children to take turns playing a game and to help each other. Encourages making associations of 1 item to another and introduces the idea of pairs or sets, a skill needed for math activities.

WHAT YOU NEED TO MAKE IT

tagboard (10" x 10")

stickers (color dots, shapes or pictures)

heavy cardboard or plastic

scissors* or Exacto knife*

clear contact

awl or nail

marker

1/2 pt. milk cartons (4)

plain paper

large brass fastener

bowl

HOW TO MAKE IT

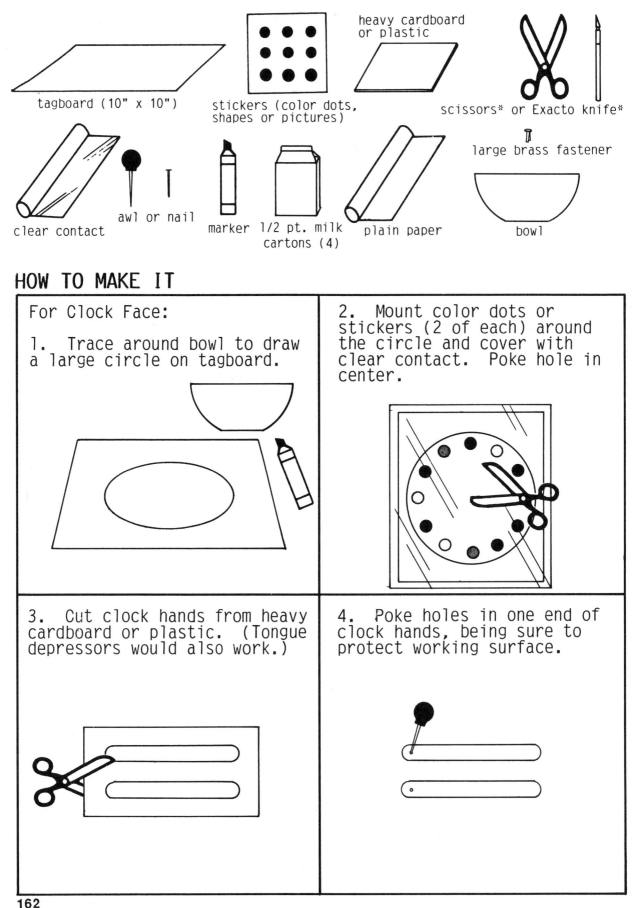

For Clock Face:

1. Trace around bowl to draw a large circle on tagboard.

2. Mount color dots or stickers (2 of each) around the circle and cover with clear contact. Poke hole in center.

3. Cut clock hands from heavy cardboard or plastic. (Tongue depressors would also work.)

4. Poke holes in one end of clock hands, being sure to protect working surface.

5. Insert brass fastener through holes in clock hands and clock face. Fold on back of clock board; leaving fairly loose so hands move easily

For Dice:

1. Cut tops off milk cartons at same place.

2. For each die, insert 1 open edge of milk carton inside the other open edge. This forms a solid square.

3. Wrap with plain paper as you would wrap a package.

4. Mount stickers, dots or shapes on each exposed surface. (Be sure you use 1 each of those used on clock face for each die).

5. Cover dice with clear contact, if desired.

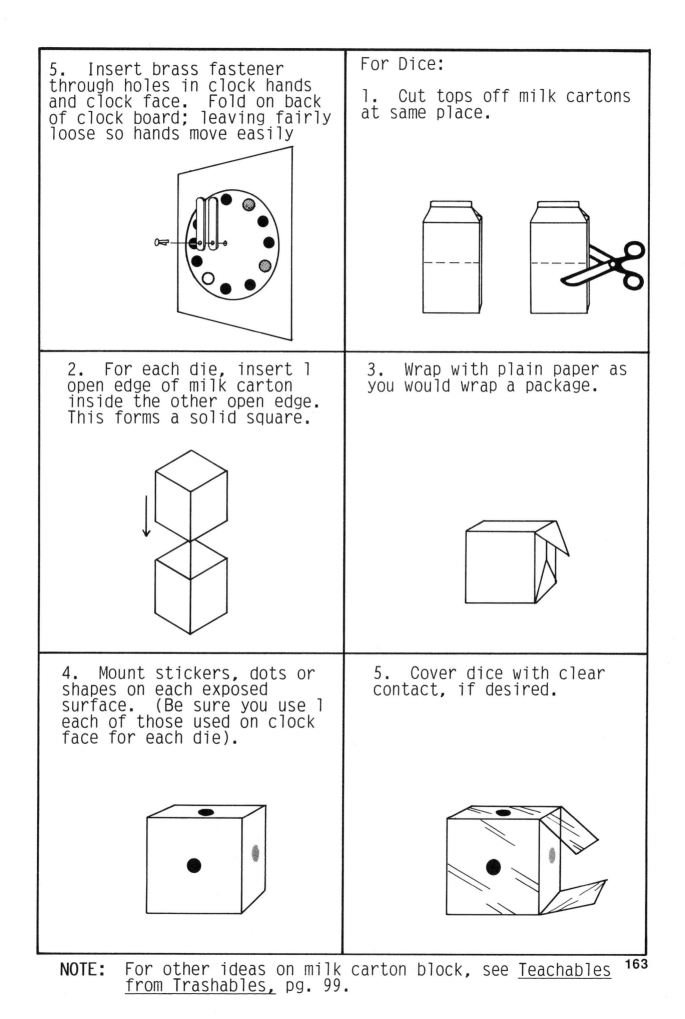

NOTE: For other ideas on milk carton block, see <u>Teachables</u> <u>from Trashables,</u> pg. 99.

Picture Partners

HOW TO USE IT

Use as a game for 2 or 3 children. Place cards face down on table. One child turns 2 cards over so pictures can be seen. If they match, child collects the pair and takes another turn. If they don't match, the cards are turned face down in the exact spot and the turn ends. Repeat until all cards are paired and collected. Adult will need to play initially to introduce game and turn-taking process and to encourage children to remember where cards are. A simple game for younger children is to spread cards out picture side up and let each child collect 1 pair for each turn. Can also be used as an individual activity in which child arranges all the pictures in pairs.

WHAT IT DOES

Helps children recognize likenesses and differences in pictures. Encourages the development of observation and memory skills, increases concentration and introduces the concept of a set of items--a pre-math skill. A very popular activity for 4-year-olds, who soon learn to concentrate much better than the adults. Also encourages taking turns, following directions and logical thinking. Hint: The pairs are harder to discriminate if they are fairly similar (i.e., all flowers, cats or dogs, and easier if they are obviously different--some pairs of flowers, fruits, etc.).

WHAT YOU NEED TO MAKE IT

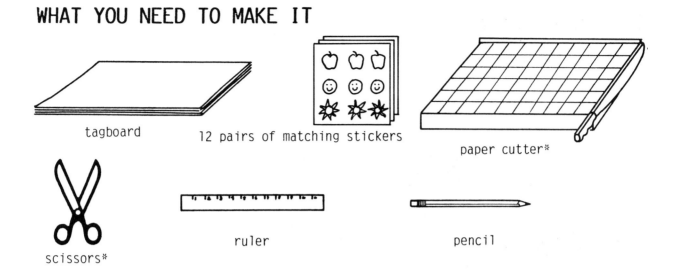

tagboard

12 pairs of matching stickers

paper cutter*

scissors*

ruler

pencil

HOW TO MAKE IT

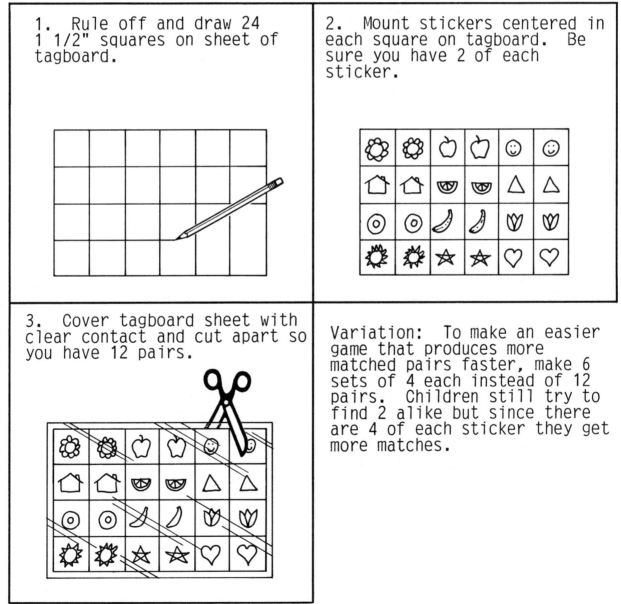

1. Rule off and draw 24 1 1/2" squares on sheet of tagboard.

2. Mount stickers centered in each square on tagboard. Be sure you have 2 of each sticker.

3. Cover tagboard sheet with clear contact and cut apart so you have 12 pairs.

Variation: To make an easier game that produces more matched pairs faster, make 6 sets of 4 each instead of 12 pairs. Children still try to find 2 alike but since there are 4 of each sticker they get more matches.

Scrambled Stickers

HOW TO USE IT

Place cards out on table with washable markers and damp sponge. Children draw lines to connect the pictures that look alike. Adults can note children's ability to recognize likenesses and differences and suggest using harder or easier cards. Adults should call attention to details and identifying characteristics in pictures to help children develop skill. When finished with 1 card, children take sponge and wipe off the lines. Make several cards at different levels of difficulty. Can be used individually or as a small group activity. Make cards in connection with any topic by using different stickers.

WHAT IT DOES

Encourages children to observe carefully to notice likenesses and differences, a pre-reading skill. By choosing some items to match that have very slight differences, children must learn to pay attention to details. Drawing the lines uses fine motor skills and also helps reinforce understanding about making comparisons and connections by having children do it themselves. Provides an activity that can be made to go with any theme. Can use letters or numbers for matching also.

WHAT YOU NEED TO MAKE IT

2 each of a variety of
stickers
(about 10 stickers per card)

5 1/2" x 8" file cards or
tagboard

clear contact paper

washable markers
or crayons

small sponges in bowl

box to hold materials

HOW TO MAKE IT

1. Mount stickers in 2 parallel columns along sides of card, leaving about 2 1/2" to 3" space between the rows.

2. Make several different cards. Vary difficulty by making some with very slight differences, and others more obvious.

3. Cover with contact.

4. Place a set of 5 or 6 cards, markers and bowl with sponge together for easy use.

NOTE: For very young children, place matching stickers within 1 to 2 spaces of each other.

STYROFOAM

Airplane

HOW TO USE IT

Older preschoolers can make these and take them outside to fly. Encourage children to press HARD as they trace parts onto Styrofoam. Cut out and assemble. Adults should assist with making the slits for the wings and inserting them to avoid ripping. Show children pictures of new and old airplanes, and talk about what they look like, names of parts and how they've changed. Think about how they fly. Use this finger play verse to add to discussion:

Airplanes fly so very high (look-up)
Jet propelled into the sky (move arms up quickly)
Roar like the wind above tree and cloud (make noise)
I wish their engines weren't so loud (cover ears)

WHAT IT DOES

Can help illustrate and teach about the principles of flying. Logical thinking is encouraged by experimenting with plane construction. Vary the size, number, and placement of wings to see how that affects flight. Also change the paper clip. Provides a fun craft activity to use in studying about transportation. Tracing and cutting encourages fine motor development. Finger plays and discussion about planes encourage language development and memory skills.

WHAT YOU NEED TO MAKE IT

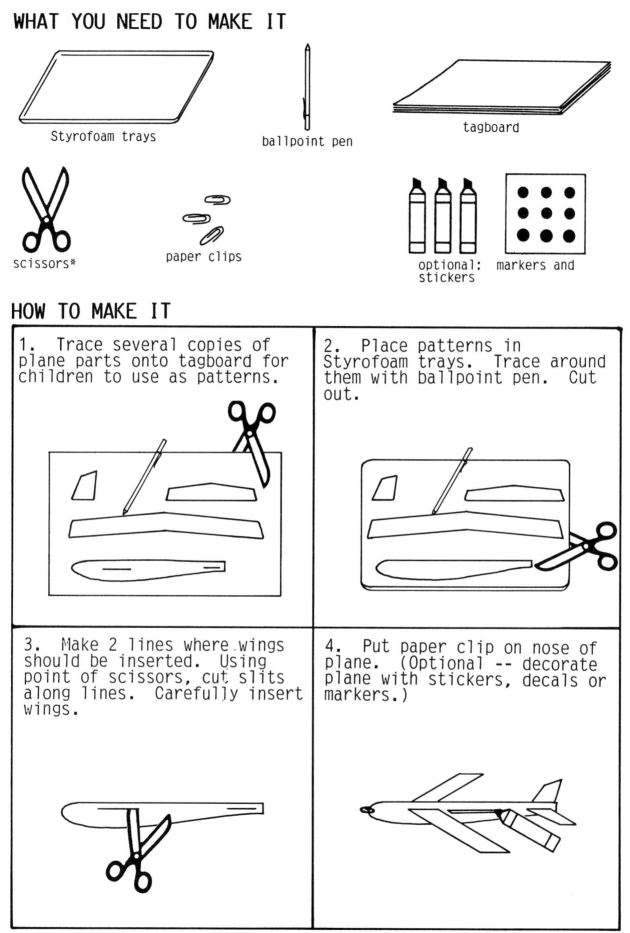

Styrofoam trays

ballpoint pen

tagboard

scissors*

paper clips

optional: markers and
stickers

HOW TO MAKE IT

1. Trace several copies of plane parts onto tagboard for children to use as patterns.

2. Place patterns in Styrofoam trays. Trace around them with ballpoint pen. Cut out.

3. Make 2 lines where wings should be inserted. Using point of scissors, cut slits along lines. Carefully insert wings.

4. Put paper clip on nose of plane. (Optional -- decorate plane with stickers, decals or markers.)

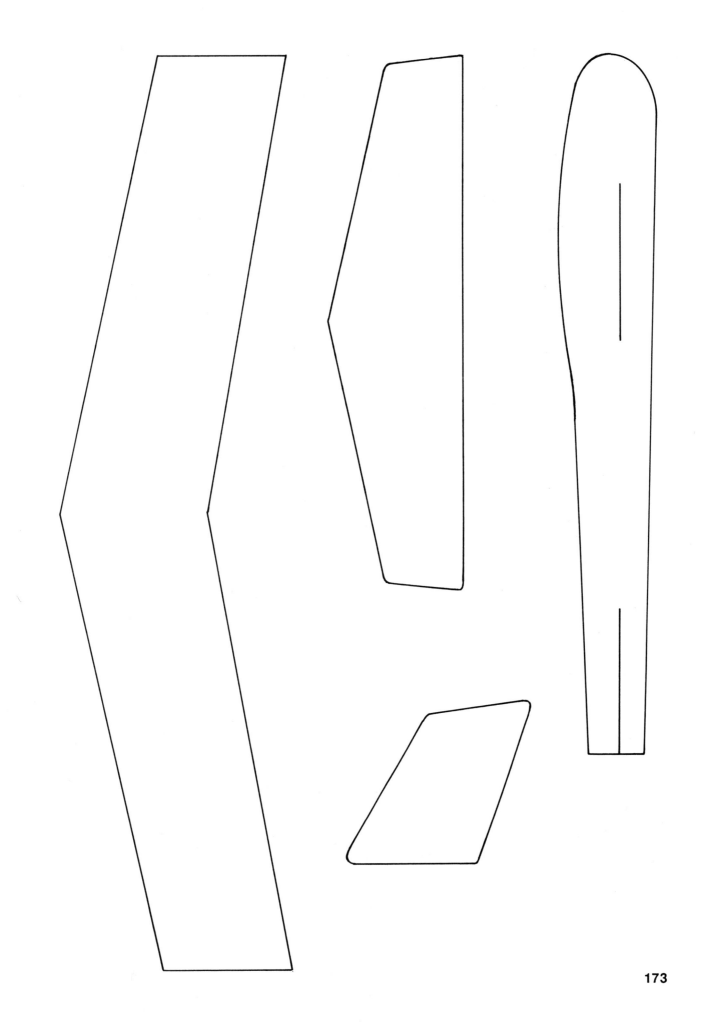

173

Egg Carton Creatures

HOW TO USE IT

Preschool children can make these to play with or to use in a display. Talk about identifying characteristics of animals or insects (i.e.: shape of ears, kind of tails, etc.). Provide sections of egg cartons and a variety of materials for decorating and allow children to make their own creatures. Make up stories about the creatures and use to act out, set up scenes or write stories. Encourage children to use creativity in making up imaginary creatures as well. Adults may need to offer assistance in folding and taping standing creatures and in pre-cutting ear shapes.

WHAT IT DOES

Constructing the creatures encourages eye-hand coordination and small motor development. Identifying characteristics of animals or insects builds vocabularies and knowledge base. Putting parts together to form the animals also encourages thinking and problem solving. Making up stories about the creatures encourages use of imagination and development of language and pre-writing skills, as well as encouraging creativity and playfulness.

WHAT YOU NEED TO MAKE IT

colorful egg cartons

construction paper

scissors*

tape

pipe cleaners

cotton

markers

bits of straw or telephone wire

glue stick

coding dots

HOW TO MAKE IT

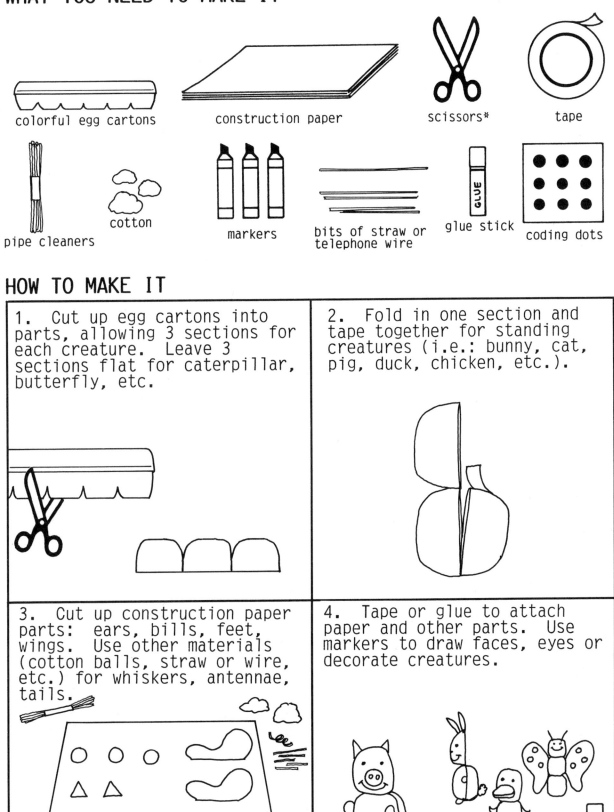

1. Cut up egg cartons into parts, allowing 3 sections for each creature. Leave 3 sections flat for caterpillar, butterfly, etc.

2. Fold in one section and tape together for standing creatures (i.e.: bunny, cat, pig, duck, chicken, etc.).

3. Cut up construction paper parts: ears, bills, feet, wings. Use other materials (cotton balls, straw or wire, etc.) for whiskers, antennae, tails.

4. Tape or glue to attach paper and other parts. Use markers to draw faces, eyes or decorate creatures.

Playing Hooky

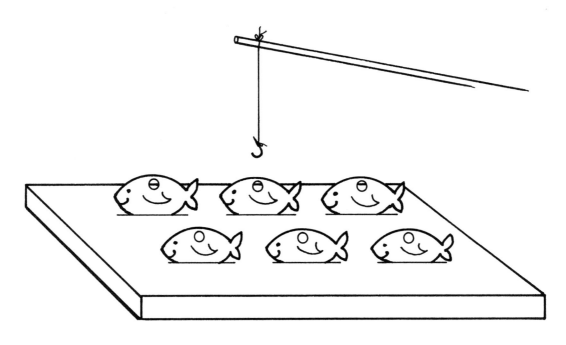

HOW TO USE IT

Children try to catch fish by hooking and lifting them with their "fishing pole". Start with short string on the pole and lengthen it as children gain skill. Talk about ways to master a difficult task and feelings involved.

Adapt the game for color, number, letter or object recognition by paper clipping to the fish pictures, dots, color strips, letters, etc. Children can identify the fish they catch, or can "go fishing" for a particular fish identified by another child. Also use in pretend play about fishing. Make several trays of fish and put in a large box or under a table. Without looking, children try to catch fish.

WHAT IT DOES

Helps develop eye-hand coordination, visual perceptual motor skills and provides practice in developing patience and control in learning a motor task. Offers an opportunity to talk about feelings like frustration and needing to try again and again. With adult assistance, can help children learn persistence. As a prop in dramatic play, can encourage use of imagination and language development. Game use encourages cognitive development, turn taking, following directions.

WHAT YOU NEED TO MAKE IT

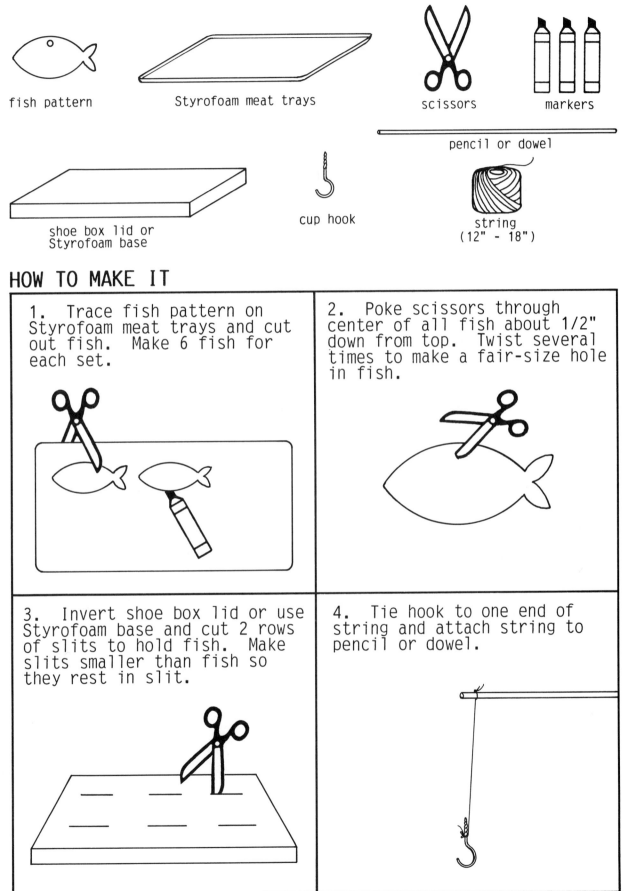

fish pattern

Styrofoam meat trays

scissors

markers

pencil or dowel

shoe box lid or
Styrofoam base

cup hook

string
(12" - 18")

HOW TO MAKE IT

1. Trace fish pattern on Styrofoam meat trays and cut out fish. Make 6 fish for each set.

2. Poke scissors through center of all fish about 1/2" down from top. Twist several times to make a fair-size hole in fish.

3. Invert shoe box lid or use Styrofoam base and cut 2 rows of slits to hold fish. Make slits smaller than fish so they rest in slit.

4. Tie hook to one end of string and attach string to pencil or dowel.

Puppet Stand

HOW TO USE IT

Encourage children to keep puppets on stands, one puppet for each dowel. Use stands with different size dowels for larger and smaller puppets. Make a game of matching puppet size to stand size -- with a very small stand for finger puppets. Children can talk to, play with and arrange puppets on the stands in special ways, imagining and discussing which puppets live next to each other, etc. Children can sort puppets by type--animal puppets on one stand, Sesame Street people puppets on another, etc.

WHAT IT DOES

Provides an inexpensive, attractive way to display puppets, making them more inviting and useful for play. Helps keep the puppets in better shape by providing convenient storage. (Stuffed away in a bag or box, puppets become unattractive and are not used as often.)

WHAT YOU NEED TO MAKE IT

round piece of styrofoam, 2" high, 8" in diameter

2 circles of cardboard, same size as styrofoam

contact paper

wooden dowels (4 or 5 per stand--about 7" high, but size can vary)

scissors*

glue

HOW TO MAKE IT

1. Glue cardboard circles to the styrofoam, one on top, and one on bottom.

2. Cover entirely with contact paper.

3. Use scissors to puncture 4 or 5 holes in upper cardboard. Carefully plan dowel placement to allow room for puppets to balance on stand.

4. Press the dowels through the upper cardboard into the styrofoam. <u>Do not go through lower cardboard.</u>

Ring the Blades

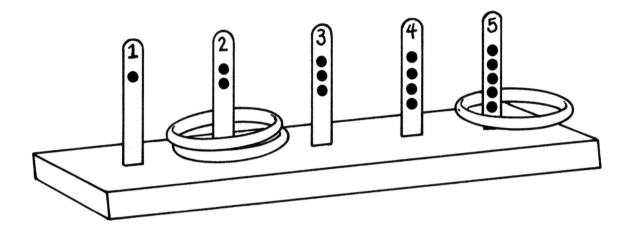

HOW TO USE IT

Can be used as an individual activity or as a small group game. Children put the appropriate number of rings on each blade. With 2 or more children, they take turns picking rings and deciding where to put them until each blade has the correct number.

Variations: 1. Add cue cards which have specific numbers or dots on them to use in the game. Children pick a card, then put rings on the blade indicated on the card. 2. Older children can play ring toss using 3 or 4 rings to toss at the blades (vary distance with ability). Use poker chips to keep score by putting into a paper cup 1 chip for each dot on the blade.

WHAT IT DOES

Teaches the relationship of numerals to the quantity they represent (1-to-1 number correspondence), a prerequisite to understanding and using number concepts. Provides practice in playing a simple game, following directions and taking turns. Ring toss game helps children learn about visual-spatial relations and how to adjust their actions to a target. Also provides practice in eye-hand coordination and an introduction to the concept of scoring.

WHAT YOU NEED TO MAKE IT

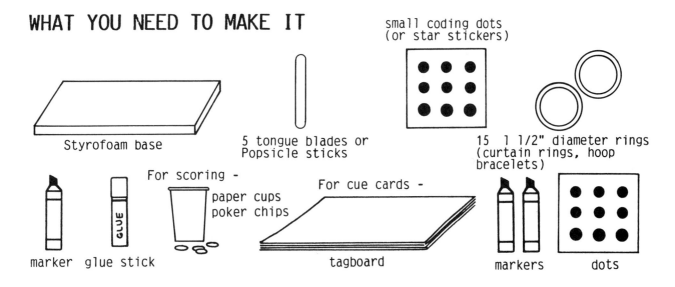

small coding dots
(or star stickers)

Styrofoam base

5 tongue blades or
Popsicle sticks

15 1 1/2" diameter rings
(curtain rings, hoop
bracelets)

marker   glue stick

For scoring -
paper cups
poker chips

For cue cards -

tagboard

markers   dots

HOW TO MAKE IT

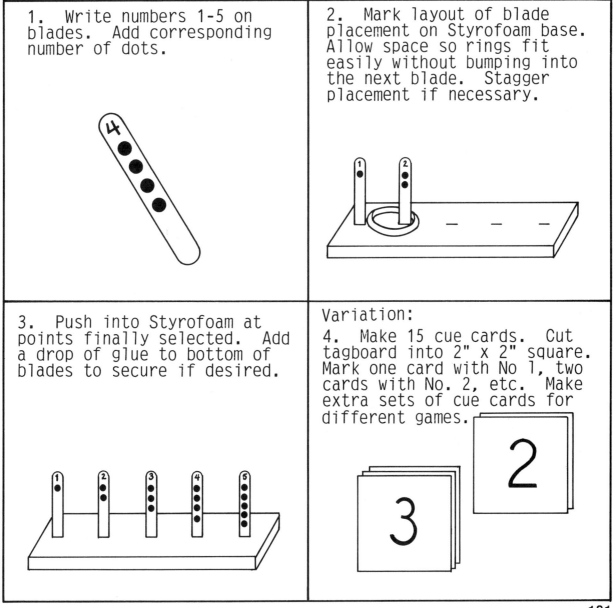

1.   Write numbers 1-5 on blades. Add corresponding number of dots.

2.   Mark layout of blade placement on Styrofoam base. Allow space so rings fit easily without bumping into the next blade. Stagger placement if necessary.

3.   Push into Styrofoam at points finally selected. Add a drop of glue to bottom of blades to secure if desired.

Variation:

4.   Make 15 cue cards. Cut tagboard into 2" x 2" square. Mark one card with No 1, two cards with No. 2, etc. Make extra sets of cue cards for different games.

Tray Tie-Ups

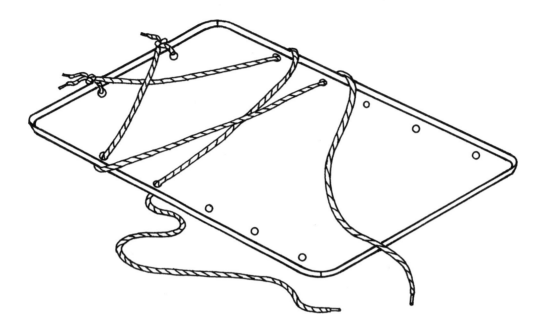

HOW TO USE IT

Children use to practice lacing. Younger children (older toddlers) can use as a simple sewing card and just insert laces in and out of holes at random. Older children can use to make designs or to practice lacing for shoes. Use 2 different color laces to teach crossover lacing. Explain the need to cross the "red" lace over the "blue" one to opposite hole, etc. Continue crossover pattern down the frame. Can also use to practice tying. Make several so more than one child can use at a time, allowing them to socialize, observe, and help each other.

WHAT IT DOES

Provides an easy-to-use frame that gives children practice in lacing and tying. Helps with the small motor and eye-hand coordination needed for sewing, lacing and stringing tasks. Provides practice in sequencing and following directions needed to lace shoes. Gives children a chance to practice a self-help skill in an easy-to-handle way.

WHAT YOU NEED TO MAKE IT

Styrofoam meat trays, any size

hole punch

2 long laces (different colors for each tray) or yarn

cellophane tape

HOW TO MAKE IT

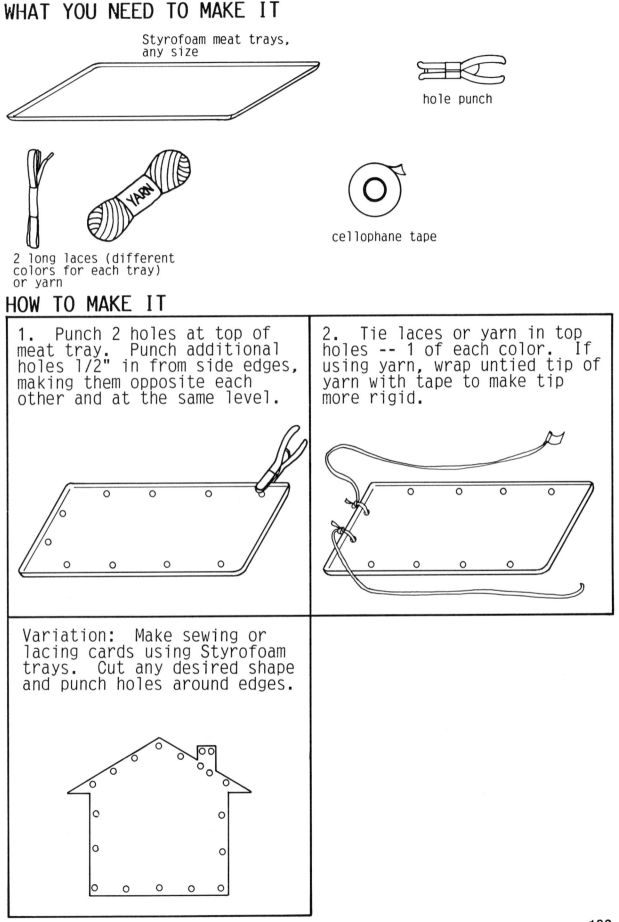

1.   Punch 2 holes at top of meat tray. Punch additional holes 1/2" in from side edges, making them opposite each other and at the same level.

2.   Tie laces or yarn in top holes -- 1 of each color. If using yarn, wrap untied tip of yarn with tape to make tip more rigid.

Variation: Make sewing or lacing cards using Styrofoam trays. Cut any desired shape and punch holes around edges.

WOOD

Keys for Learning

HOW TO USE IT

Prop hook board up against wall and place key outline card on it. Give child ring of keys for that card. Encourage child to look at the keys carefully and try them out next to the outlines. Point out the different wiggley lines along one edge and the shape of the top and bottom of the keys. Children place keys that match the outline on the hooks. Younger children (2-3) will enjoy placing the keys on the hooks and will ignore matching shapes although they could match keys of different colors to colored outlines. Older children may still need encouragement to look for the correct match. Can make several cards for different sets of keys. If you do this, make one master guide for key placement.

WHAT IT DOES

Putting keys on hooks develops eye-hand coordination and fine motor skills. Children love to play with keys and this gives them an interesting thing to do with them. Matching the key shapes provides a difficult and challenging perceptual task for older preschoolers.

HINT: If making multiple sets, place the 6 keys for each card on a different color large plastic paper clip or Discovery Toy ring. Code the outline card with same color as the ring so you and the children know which keys go to which card. Putting keys on and taking them off the rings also helps develop fine motor skills.

WHAT YOU NEED TO MAKE IT

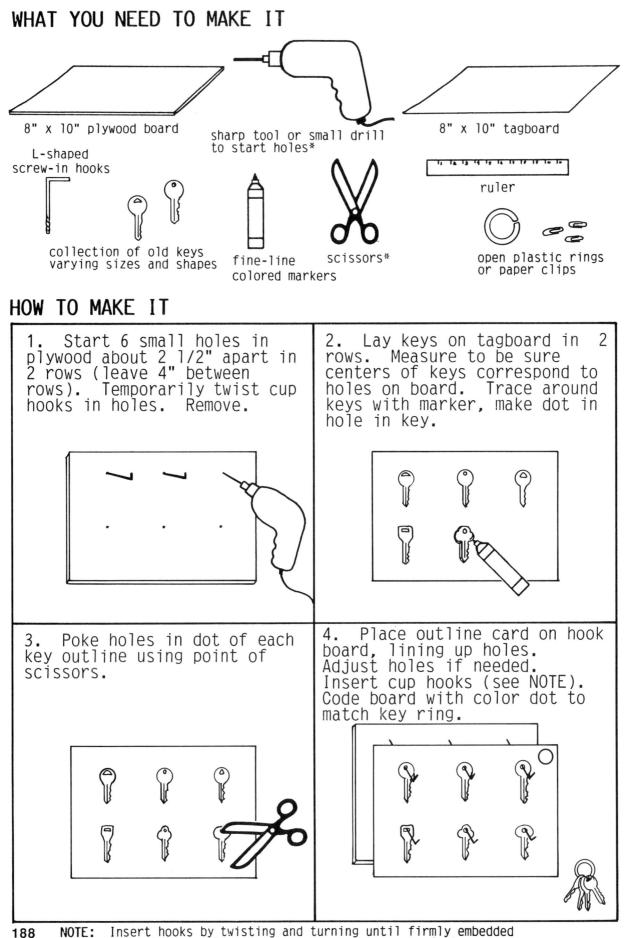

8" x 10" plywood board

sharp tool or small drill to start holes*

8" x 10" tagboard

L-shaped screw-in hooks

collection of old keys varying sizes and shapes

fine-line colored markers

scissors*

ruler

open plastic rings or paper clips

HOW TO MAKE IT

1. Start 6 small holes in plywood about 2 1/2" apart in 2 rows (leave 4" between rows). Temporarily twist cup hooks in holes. Remove.

2. Lay keys on tagboard in 2 rows. Measure to be sure centers of keys correspond to holes on board. Trace around keys with marker, make dot in hole in key.

3. Poke holes in dot of each key outline using point of scissors.

4. Place outline card on hook board, lining up holes. Adjust holes if needed. Insert cup hooks (see NOTE). Code board with color dot to match key ring.

188 NOTE: Insert hooks by twisting and turning until firmly embedded in plywood. Be sure they do not go through to back of plywood.

Nailboard Designs

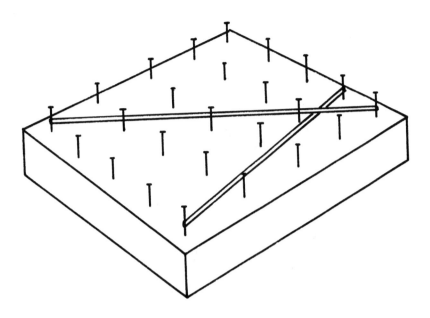

HOW TO USE IT

Children stretch rubber bands from nail to nail in various directions, forming different designs. Can twist and turn rubber band to form various clusters or practice weaving patterns with the rubber bands. Children can make up their own designs and can try to follow patterns suggested by drawing designs on cards or can use in particular number tasks (i.e.: "Make all the rubber bands circle 4 nails." Encourage children to make a variety of shapes of different sizes and talk about them.

WHAT IT DOES

Stimulates creativity and imagination. Teaches eye-hand, finger coordination and provides practice in using fine motor skills. Can also help teach following directions or counting when used with pattern cards. Provides practice in manipulating sizes and shapes, and observing characteristics of different shapes.

WHAT YOU NEED TO MAKE IT

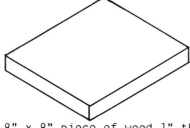

8" x 8" piece of wood 1" thick

25 2" nails

1 package of colored and assorted size rubber bands

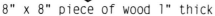

ruler

sandpaper

hammer*

HOW TO MAKE IT

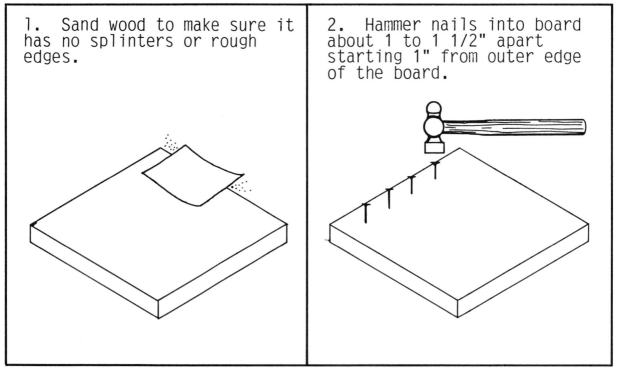

1. Sand wood to make sure it has no splinters or rough edges.

2. Hammer nails into board about 1 to 1 1/2" apart starting 1" from outer edge of the board.

NOTE: Can make larger boards using more nails if you wish - 100-nail boards are very useful for teaching number concepts (10 rows of 10 nails each). Can also be made using the styrofoam/cardboard combination suggested in the Puppet Stand (pg. 178), but the nails will not hold as firmly for prolonged use.

Pegboard Pictures

HOW TO USE IT

Put out boards and long laces for children to use. For easier lacing, leather or plastic-coated laces may be used. Tie knot at one end. Pull the lace through one hole near picture corner to get started and demonstrate poking lace through holes along outline going back and forth from front to back of board. Younger children may lace in random fashion and not follow outline, which is fine. Talk about the pictures on the board, naming the various parts (roof, chimney, etc.), and also concepts such as inside, outside, front, back, etc.

WHAT IT DOES

Provides desirable, sturdy lacing boards which will last much longer than cardboard sewing cards. Lacing encourages eye-hand coordination, small motor development and problem solving. Talking about pictures and concepts expands vocabularies and encourages language development.

WHAT YOU NEED TO MAKE IT

9" square sections of pegboard

coloring book pictures

paper

pencil

scissors*

markers or paint

spray paint (optional)

HOW TO MAKE IT

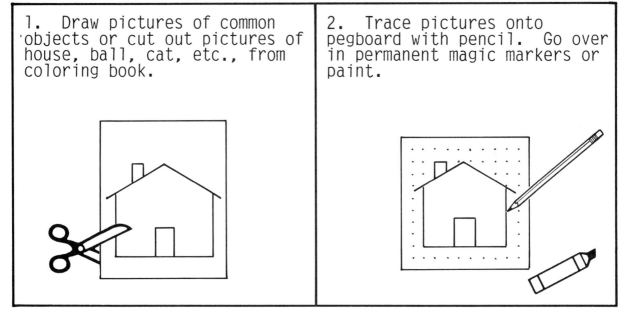

1. Draw pictures of common objects or cut out pictures of house, ball, cat, etc., from coloring book.

2. Trace pictures onto pegboard with pencil. Go over in permanent magic markers or paint.

NOTE: If desired, pegboards could be spray painted white before picture outlines are added.

WRAPPING PAPER

Look-Alikes

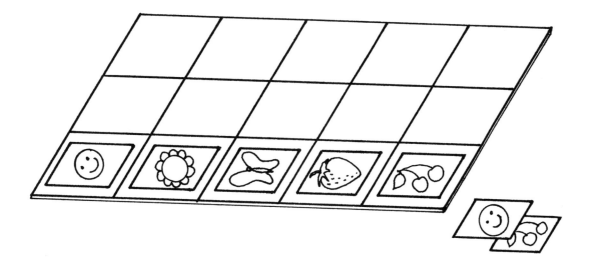

HOW TO USE IT

Children complete each row with the pictures that match. Can be played by 1 or 2 children. Place all the small cards face down on the table. Children take turns picking a card and finding the place where it belongs. Continue until all the cards are used up and the rows complete. Wrapping paper pictures or designs that are very similar can be used to make the game more difficult for older preschoolers. Variation: Cards can be used alone to play a game like Old Maid; picking cards from each other to make pairs.

WHAT IT DOES

Encourages children to look for similarities and differences in pictures and to pay attention to details. Provides practice in working from left to right. Helps develop concentration, memory and interest in finishing a task, all of which are reading readiness skills. Also offers a simple, non-competitive game to help teach taking turns. Picture identification and matching on board can be done by 2 1/2 to 3-year-olds. Pattern discrimination games are suitable for 4 to 5-year-olds.

WHAT YOU NEED TO MAKE IT

suitable wrapping paper   glue   marker   5" x 8" file cards

ruler   scissors*   clear contact

HOW TO MAKE IT

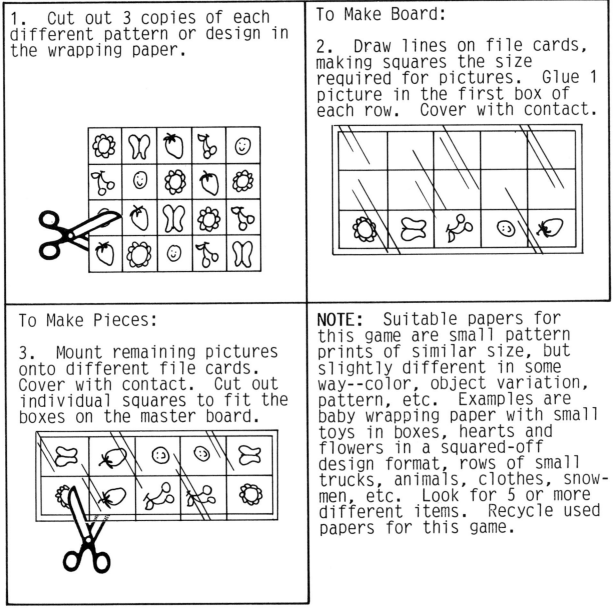

1.   Cut out 3 copies of each different pattern or design in the wrapping paper.

To Make Board:

2.   Draw lines on file cards, making squares the size required for pictures. Glue 1 picture in the first box of each row. Cover with contact.

To Make Pieces:

3.   Mount remaining pictures onto different file cards. Cover with contact. Cut out individual squares to fit the boxes on the master board.

NOTE: Suitable papers for this game are small pattern prints of similar size, but slightly different in some way--color, object variation, pattern, etc. Examples are baby wrapping paper with small toys in boxes, hearts and flowers in a squared-off design format, rows of small trucks, animals, clothes, snowmen, etc. Look for 5 or more different items. Recycle used papers for this game.

Paper Puzzlers

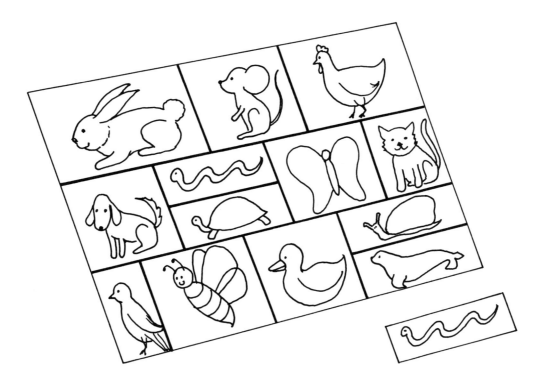

HOW TO USE IT

As an independent activity, children match the individual pictures to those on the master board. As a small group activity, adult distributes pictures to a few children and places the master board in center of group. Adult asks questions which describe pictures on the board and child holding the card matching that description puts it on the board. Questions can be very simple ones asking for a specific object or more difficult ones requiring the child to think about the pictures. Examples: For wrapping paper of trucks or vehicles -- "Who has a truck that carries loads of dirt?" or "Who has the dump truck?" For Sesame Street character paper -- "Who has Oscar?" or "Who has the character who lives in a very strange place?

WHAT IT DOES

Helps children recognize likenesses and differences and learn about ways of classifying things. Helps the development of language and thinking skills as well as ability to listen and follow directions. Games can be made to relate to as many topics as there are pictures on assorted wrapping paper. All types of animals, toys, vehicles, flowers, rocket ships, desserts, school or party scenes are available.

WHAT YOU NEED TO MAKE IT

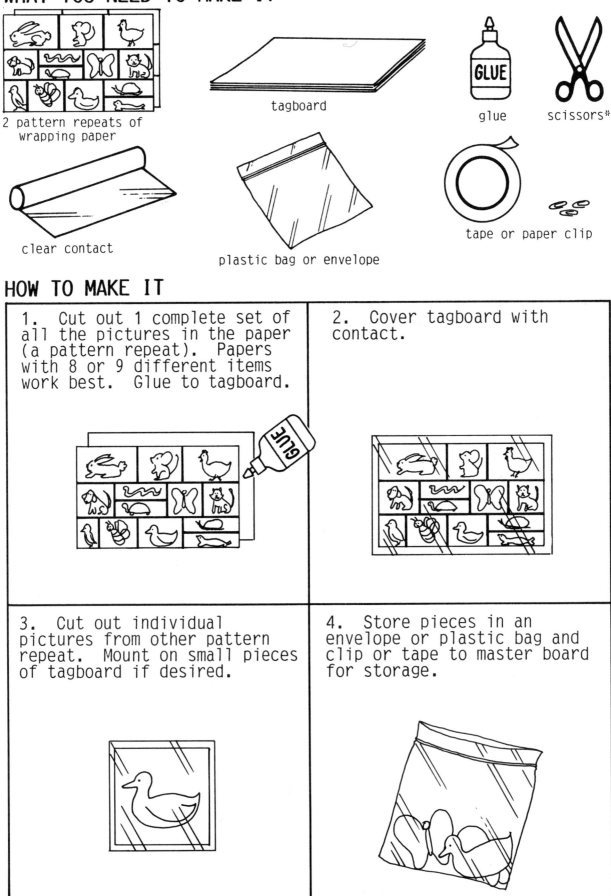

2 pattern repeats of
wrapping paper

tagboard

glue

scissors*

clear contact

plastic bag or envelope

tape or paper clip

HOW TO MAKE IT

1. Cut out 1 complete set of all the pictures in the paper (a pattern repeat). Papers with 8 or 9 different items work best. Glue to tagboard.

2. Cover tagboard with contact.

3. Cut out individual pictures from other pattern repeat. Mount on small pieces of tagboard if desired.

4. Store pieces in an envelope or plastic bag and clip or tape to master board for storage.

198 NOTE: For hints on wrapping paper selection, see the Introduction.

Simple Lotto

HOW TO USE IT

Children match the individual pictures to those on the master board. Can be used by one child as a puzzle or played like lotto for 3 or 4 children. Place individual cards face down in a pile. Give each player a master board. Children take turns picking cards and looking to see where the object belongs. Let the child who picks the card be the main searcher but encourage all the children to help "find it". Continue playing until all cards are covered. Do not stress the idea of being first to have a board covered. Emphasize the group process and keep everyone involved.

WHAT IT DOES

Teaches recognition of likenesses and differences. Matching pictures or patterns helps children learn visual discrimination, a pre-reading skill. Provides opportunities for taking turns and for cooperative game-playing.

Master boards with 3 or 4 pictures on them can be used as a simple game for 2 or 3 younger children (2-3). For older children, make master boards with 6 pictures on them.

WHAT YOU NEED TO MAKE IT

gift wrapping paper with individual pictures

8 8" x 5" unlined file cards or tagboard

scissors*

glue

ruler

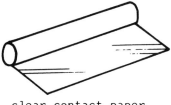
black marker

clear contact paper

HOW TO MAKE IT

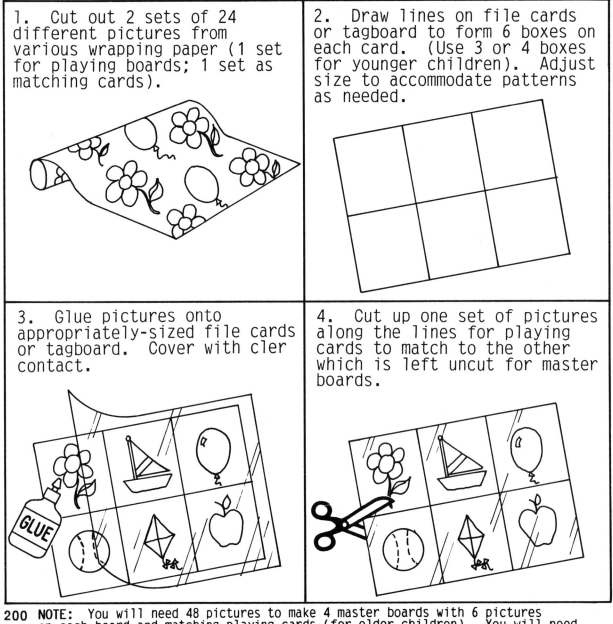

1. Cut out 2 sets of 24 different pictures from various wrapping paper (1 set for playing boards; 1 set as matching cards).

2. Draw lines on file cards or tagboard to form 6 boxes on each card. (Use 3 or 4 boxes for younger children). Adjust size to accommodate patterns as needed.

3. Glue pictures onto appropriately-sized file cards or tagboard. Cover with cler contact.

4. Cut up one set of pictures along the lines for playing cards to match to the other which is left uncut for master boards.

200 **NOTE:** You will need 48 pictures to make 4 master boards with 6 pictures on each board and matching playing cards (for older children). You will need 24 pictures to make 4 sets with 3 pictures on each card for younger children.

MISCELLANEOUS

Easy Flannelboard

HOW TO USE IT

Use as an individual flannel or felt board, in both traditional as well as unique ways. Retell favorite stories with cut-out characters, use as a counting activity matching objects to numerals, or spell names and words with felt letters. Individually, children can make pictures or designs with cutouts provided. As a group activity, adult can provide specific directions to follow (i.e., put 5 yellow circles on your board; see if you can find some shapes that make a house; put a tree next to the house, etc.).

WHAT IT DOES

Flannel boards offer children a variety of manipulative, sensory and creative experiences. Making design pictures fosters creativity and understanding of design concepts. Counting out objects to match numbers helps teach about the meaning of numbers. Playing with letters helps children learn to recognize and become familiar with letters. Retelling stories helps develop memory skills, understanding of sequencing and language concepts.

WHAT YOU NEED TO MAKE IT

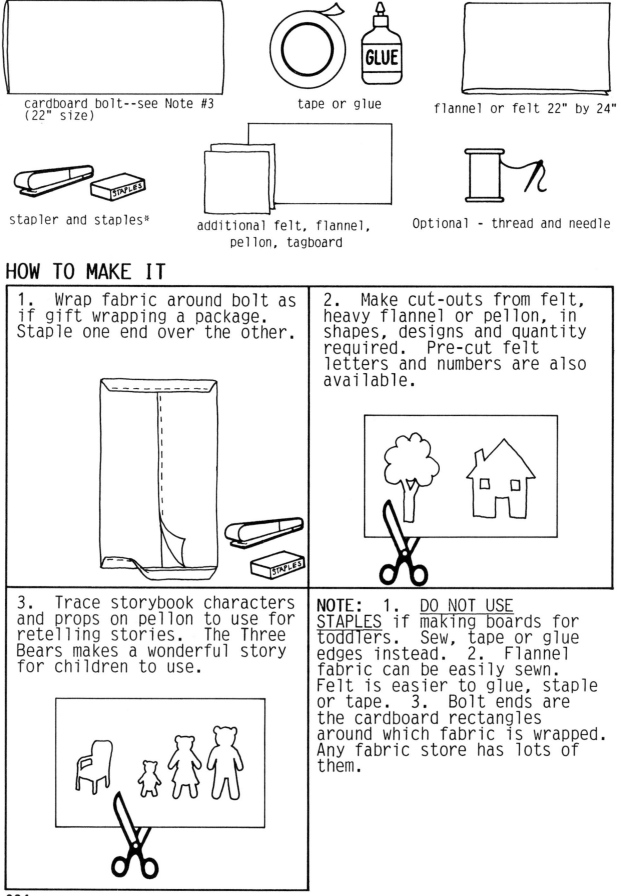

cardboard bolt--see Note #3
(22" size)

tape or glue

flannel or felt 22" by 24"

stapler and staples*

additional felt, flannel,
pellon, tagboard

Optional - thread and needle

HOW TO MAKE IT

1. Wrap fabric around bolt as if gift wrapping a package. Staple one end over the other.

2. Make cut-outs from felt, heavy flannel or pellon, in shapes, designs and quantity required. Pre-cut felt letters and numbers are also available.

3. Trace storybook characters and props on pellon to use for retelling stories. The Three Bears makes a wonderful story for children to use.

NOTE: 1. <u>DO NOT USE STAPLES</u> if making boards for toddlers. Sew, tape or glue edges instead. 2. Flannel fabric can be easily sewn. Felt is easier to glue, staple or tape. 3. Bolt ends are the cardboard rectangles around which fabric is wrapped. Any fabric store has lots of them.

Gas Pump

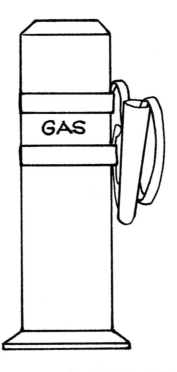

HOW TO USE IT

An excellent "make-it" project for older pre-schoolers and schoolagers. Collect several toothpaste pumps and ask children to think of things to make from them (i.e.: rockets, silos). Show the gas pump materials as well. Discuss ways of attaching the parts. Let the children make the things they would like. Encourage them to help each other and assist as needed. All creations can be used in the block corner when building cities, roads, etc. The gas pumps can also be used with small cars to "fill'er up!"

WHAT IT DOES

Provides children with something they can make to use in their play. Good to use in connection with a field trip to a service station or in studying about transportation. Can stimulate ideas for block building. Constructing the pumps uses fine motor skills and provides practice in planning and following directions. Offers an example of creating "props" from common objects to use in imaginative ways.

WHAT YOU NEED TO MAKE IT

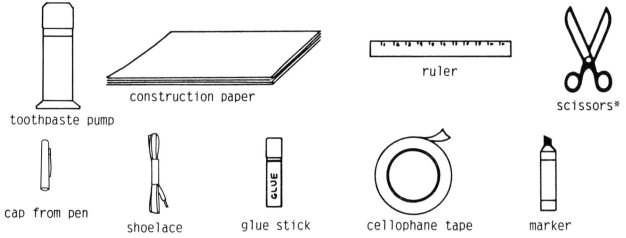

toothpaste pump

construction paper

ruler

scissors*

cap from pen

shoelace

glue stick

cellophane tape

marker

HOW TO MAKE IT

1. Measure and cut pieces of construction paper to fit around pump, allowing overlap for easy gluing. Wrap paper and glue.

2. Hold pen cap next to pump above middle and attach with tape, running tape around pump and through metal or plastic protrusion on cap.

3. Tape shoelace to pump above pen cap. Again run tape around pump and one end of lace.

4. Decorate pump with marker. Print "GAS" or draw dials and numbers.

Kool-Aid Playdough

HOW TO USE IT

Children roll, knead, pat, shape, cut, poke and create things from cookies to creatures. Extend playful uses with props such as round blocks or rolling pins, cookie cutters, molds, muffin tins, etc. Make various colors for special times of year. Make one color at a time, or if two colors are used and will be mixed, make ones that will create a new color (i.e.: yellow and red will turn orange).

WHAT IT DOES

Making the play dough is a fun group activity offering opportunities to measure, mix, follow directions, read a recipe, etc. Using the play dough stimulates children's creativity, provides practice in using fingers and hands to control and manipulate a material (fine motor skills) and offers a soothing, relaxing sensory experience.

This is the best homemade play dough available. It lasts the longest, is not grainy and smells <u>sooo</u> good!

WHAT YOU NEED TO MAKE IT

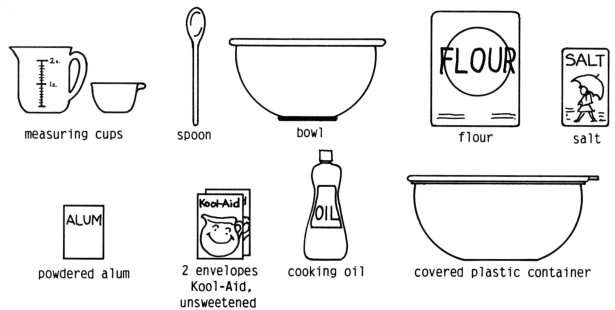

measuring cups   spoon   bowl   flour   salt

powdered alum   2 envelopes Kool-Aid, unsweetened   cooking oil   covered plastic container

HOW TO MAKE IT

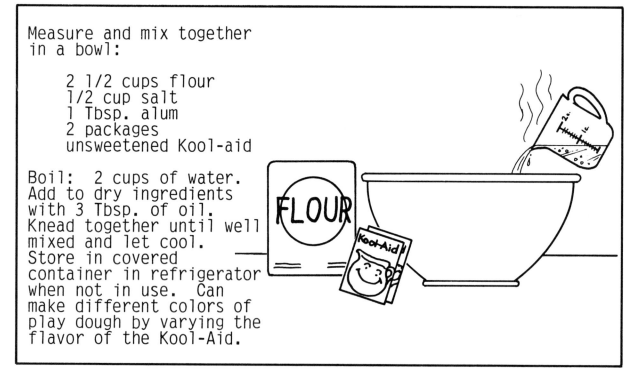

Measure and mix together
in a bowl:

    2 1/2 cups flour
    1/2 cup salt
    1 Tbsp. alum
    2 packages
    unsweetened Kool-aid

Boil: 2 cups of water.
Add to dry ingredients
with 3 Tbsp. of oil.
Knead together until well
mixed and let cool.
Store in covered
container in refrigerator
when not in use. Can
make different colors of
play dough by varying the
flavor of the Kool-Aid.

Musical Pipes

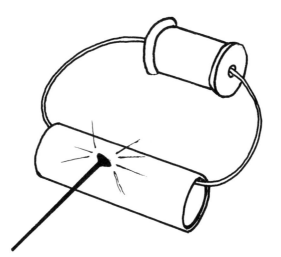

HOW TO USE IT

Children hit the pipe with the nail to produce sound.
Children can experiment using different things to strike the pipe--from wood dowels or pencils to large bolts--to see what kinds of sounds are produced. Discuss what might make sounds higher or lower, louder or softer. Experiment with striking a hand-held pipe and one that is swinging. Talk about the difference in sound (more or less resonance). Observe if striking the spool produced any sound and talk about the comparison. Use as a triangle in a rhythm band set. Encourage children to strike instruments in time to music, noting fast and slow tempos.

WHAT IT DOES

Helps children learn about how sounds are produced and what affects those sounds. Good for discussing and illustrating meanings of words associated with music and sound such as loud, soft. Provides inexpensive and easy way to make instruments to add to a rhythm band or to accompany records or singing. Observing, experimenting and noting differences introduces children to the scientific method of inquiry.

WHAT YOU NEED TO MAKE IT

2 1/2" - 3" piece of pipe

wire or string

large empty thread spool

nail

HOW TO MAKE IT

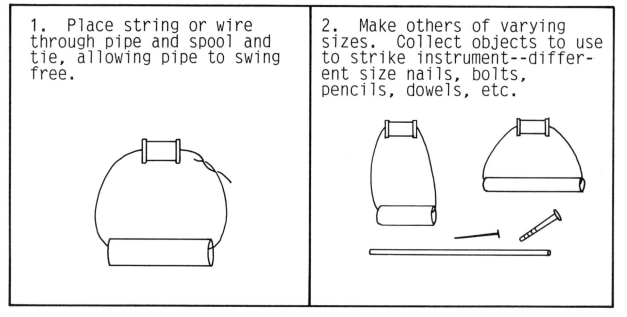

1. Place string or wire through pipe and spool and tie, allowing pipe to swing free.

2. Make others of varying sizes. Collect objects to use to strike instrument--different size nails, bolts, pencils, dowels, etc.

Poke & Peek

HOW TO USE IT

Can be used with a group of 2-4 toddlers. Adult gives each toddler an envelope containing approximately 10 round toothpicks or thin plastic cocktail stirrers. Invert the colander and let them poke the toothpicks through the holes. Talk about what the children are doing and when all the toothpicks are gone, wonder where they are! Ask the children. Pick up the colander, redistribute the same toothpicks and start all over again. After children have done this a few times, they will be able to use it independently.

WHAT IT DOES

Provides an appealing activity that encourages fine motor development and eye-hand coordination. Also provides practice with things disappearing and reappearing, an item of great interest, importance and fascination to toddlers. Provides a side-by-side play activity that children can do together without having to take turns or wait. Offers lots of opportunities for manipulation.

WHAT YOU NEED TO MAKE IT

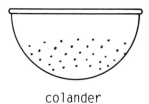

colander

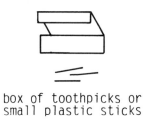

box of toothpicks or
small plastic sticks

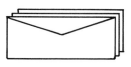

envelopes

HOW TO MAKE IT

1. Place 10-15 toothpicks in envelopes. Have at least 1 envelope for each child.	2. Put envelopes inside colander for ready access. Distribute envelopes to toddlers assembled around table or on floor.

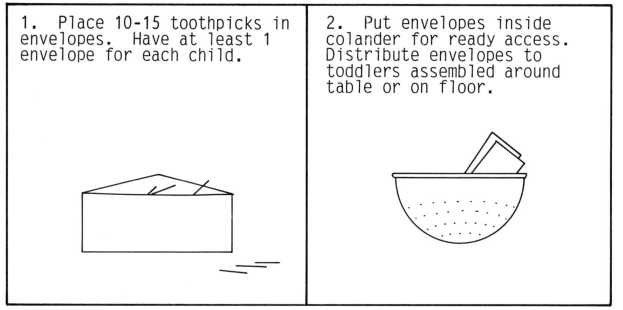

Shake a Legg

HOW TO USE IT

Children use them to keep time with records or singing. Can be used for rhythm pattern games. Adult taps or plays a rhythm pattern (1 short, 1 long, 1 short, 1 long) and has child repeat pattern with shakers. For an art activity, shakers could be covered with papier-mâché (following directions on package), allowed to dry and painted with colorful designs. Can make shakers with different contents and compare sounds.

WHAT IT DOES

Provides another instrument to add to a rhythm band or to use in a music or dramatic play interest area. Encourages children to keep time to music and to become aware of rhythmic patterns by matching them. Decorating the shakers to look like maracas provides creative and sensory-manipulative fun. When used in a unit on Spain or Mexico, can provide a starting point for discussion on ethnic musical style.

WHAT YOU NEED TO MAKE IT

Leggs Egg

3/4" wood square or dowel for handle

1 1/2" piece thin wood

cloth Mystic tape

knife*

hammer

small nail*

beans, sand, rice, etc.,
for inside

For Decorations:

PAPER MÂCHE

papier-mâché
mixture

markers

tape or paint

HOW TO MAKE IT

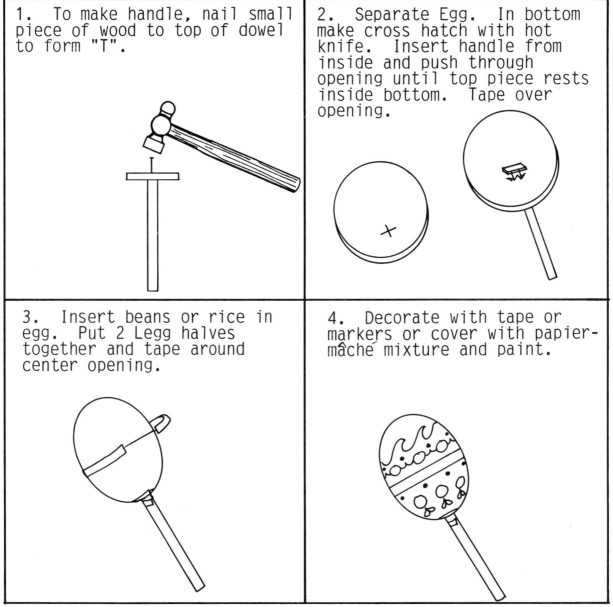

1. To make handle, nail small piece of wood to top of dowel to form "T".

2. Separate Egg. In bottom make cross hatch with hot knife. Insert handle from inside and push through opening until top piece rests inside bottom. Tape over opening.

3. Insert beans or rice in egg. Put 2 Legg halves together and tape around center opening.

4. Decorate with tape or markers or cover with papier-mâché mixture and paint.

Rings to String

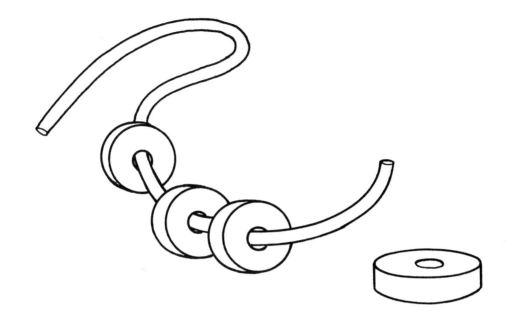

HOW TO USE IT

Children string the washers onto the plastic tubing. Put out baskets of plastic tubes and large rubber washers with large holes. After showing toddlers how to put tubing through holes in washers, let them do it independently. Make a few sets so more than 1 toddler can do this at a time. It is easy for toddlers to string washers on tubing because it stays erect and is easy to hold.

Variation: Rubber washers and tubes can also be used in the water table. Children can blow bubbles through plastic tubing.

WHAT IT DOES

Makes toddlers' first attempts at bead stringing more successful by avoiding the frustration caused by standard bead laces. Stringing teaches eye-hand coordination and control of small muscles. Provides lots of objects for toddlers to control and manipulate. Sensory development is enhanced when tubing and washers are used in the water table.

WHAT YOU NEED TO MAKE IT

plastic tubing

rubber washers
with holes

box

HOW TO MAKE IT

1. Cut tubing into 18" to 24" sections.	2. Put one washer on tube and tie loosely to form stopper.
3. Various size washers can be used, provided the tubing fits.	4. Store all material together in a small box.

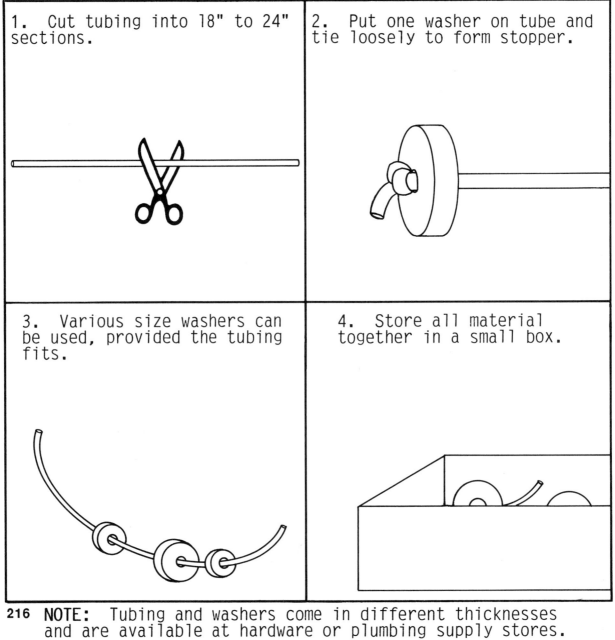

NOTE: Tubing and washers come in different thicknesses and are available at hardware or plumbing supply stores.

Rolling Art

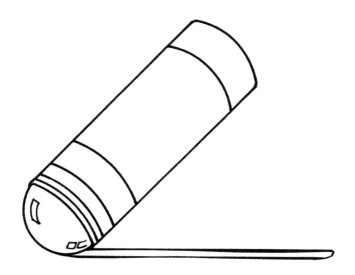

HOW TO USE IT

Put out several bottles filled with different color paints and large sheets of paper. Show children how to tilt bottles and roll them over paper to paint. Can be used by individual children or by a small group working on a large roll of shelf paper or craft paper to make a mural. Can be used indoors or as an easy, non-spill way to take paints outdoors. Replace caps on bottles after use so paints won't dry out. Best if used with larger sheets of paper so children can use larger movements and roll over any small leaks of paint from the bottle.

WHAT IT DOES

Painting with rollers encourages children to experiment with art media in a new and different way. Encourages large sweeping and swirling motions as the child rolls the bottles along. Allows experimentation with line, shape, color, color mixing and general sensory exploration. Provides a relatively non-messy way for toddlers to paint. Serves as an intermediate step between brush painting and fingerpainting.

WHAT YOU NEED TO MAKE IT

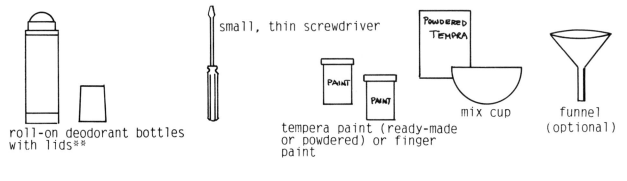

roll-on deodorant bottles
with lids**

small, thin screwdriver

POWDERED
TEMPRA

PAINT

PAINT

tempera paint (ready-made
or powdered) or finger
paint

mix cup

funnel
(optional)

HOW TO MAKE IT

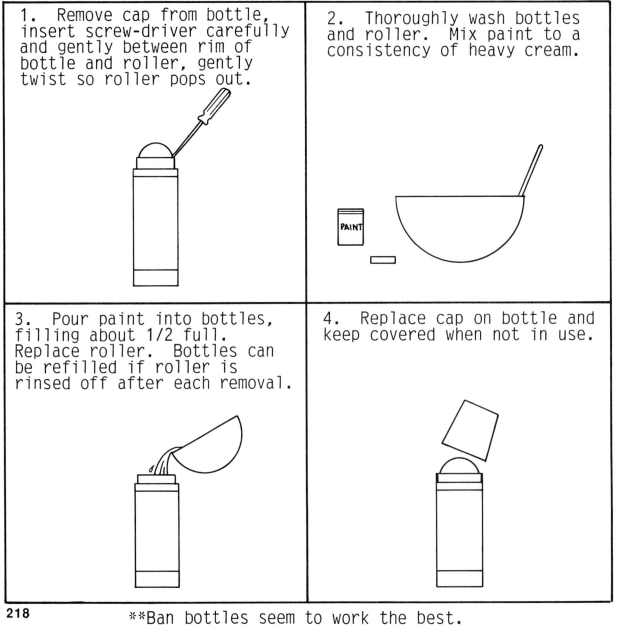

1.   Remove cap from bottle,
insert screw-driver carefully
and gently between rim of
bottle and roller, gently
twist so roller pops out.

2.   Thoroughly wash bottles
and roller. Mix paint to a
consistency of heavy cream.

3.   Pour paint into bottles,
filling about 1/2 full.
Replace roller. Bottles can
be refilled if roller is
rinsed off after each removal.

4.   Replace cap on bottle and
keep covered when not in use.

PAINT

218   **Ban bottles seem to work the best.

Simple Sorting

HOW TO USE IT

Put out muffin tin and container of small plastic beads. Children sort the beads into the cups by color, matching the bead color to the "cue color" circle in each cup.

Sorting activity can be changed by varying the liners set in the muffin tin. Liners can be made to indicate number 1-8, shapes, outlines or colors of specific items such as buttons. Some items to use for sorting are wooden beads, counting cubes, beans, buttons, pegs, plastic shapes, marbles or pieces from other games.

WHAT IT DOES

Offers a way to use common material (i.e.: beads, buttons) to teach specific concepts such as color or shape matching. Sorting tasks help children learn to recognize likenesses and differences and to organize items by catagories based on identifying characteristics. This helps children learn to pay attention to details and sharpens perceptual skills. Picking up small objects helps develop fine motor coordinaton.

WHAT YOU NEED TO MAKE IT

6-8 cup muffin tin

colored construction paper

scissors*

pencil

colored beads

container for beads

HOW TO MAKE IT

1. Trace around bottom of muffin tin on colored construction paper that closely matches color of beads. Make 1 circle of each color.

2. Cut out circles and place inside muffin tin recesses so each cup has a different color liner.

3. Fill small plastic bowl with lots of multi-colored small plastic beads.

4. Make additional sets of liners for muffin tins to use in variation games.

INDEX

PRIMARY LEARNING FOCUS

ARTS & CRAFTS

Airplane
Banjo
Egg Carton Creatures
Furry Animal Friend
Gas Pump
Hanging Planter
Kool-Aid Playdough
Nail Board Designs
Paper Bag Kickball
Rolling Art
Sizzling Rockets
Squish Bags
Tape Tube Animals
Tube Puppet Playmates

SCIENCE & NATURE

Cue Me In
Fancy Fish
Hanging Planter
Magnet Mysteries
Painter's Palette
Sizzling Rockets
Slow Motion Ocean
Squish Bag
Tape Tube Animals

NUMBER CONCEPTS

Bottle Cap Counters
Counting Circles
Cube-It
Money Matters
Numbers Galore
Numerous Numerals
Pillow Case Counters
Pizza Pin-Ups
Ring the Blade
Tic-Tac-Toe
Top the Box
What's My Number?

LANGUAGE ARTS & DRAMATIC PLAY

Banjo
Chatter Cartons
Cue Me In
Dots to Dinosaurs
Easy Flannel Board
Egg Carton Creatures
Furry Animal Friends
Milk Carton Puppet
Money Matters
Picture Partners
Playing Hooky
Puppet Stand
Quick & Easy Doll Clothes
Shoe Box Train
Take Apart People
Take Apart Teddy
Tambourine
Tape Tube Animals
Tube Puppet Playmates

COOPERATIVE GAMES

Child Size Game Net
Clock Matching
Counting Circles
Cue Me In
Numbers Galore
Picture Partners
Poke & Peek
Simple Lotto
Sociable Cracker Game
Soda Pop Drop
Stop & Go Race Game
Target Toss
Tic-Tac-Toe

MUSIC

Banjo
Musical Pipes
Shake A Legg
Tambourine

VISUAL PERCEPTION

Airplane
Bottle Cap Counters
Bucket Brigade
Clock Matching
Copycat Covers
Counting Circles
Dots to Dinosaurs
Keys for Learning
Letter Line-Up
Lids Unlimited
Look Alikes
Painter's Palette
Paper Puzzles
Picture Partners
Scrambled Stickers
Shape Finders
Simple Lotto
Simple Sorting
Sociable Cracker Game
Where's the Scoop?
Ziploc Dot-to-Dot

TODDLERS

Bucket Brigade
Chatter Cartons
Child Size Game Net
Easy Flannel Board
Furry Animal Friends
Kool-Aid Playdough
Lid-der Box
Paper Bag Kickball
Poke & Peek
Rings to String
Rolling Art
Shoe Box Train
Simple Lotto
Soap Bottle Pull Toy
Soda Pop Drop
Squish Bags
Take Apart Teddy
Twist & Turn

FINE & GROSS MOTOR

Bucket Brigade
Chatter Cartons
Child Size Game Net
Clock Matching
Copycat Covers
Keys for Learning
Lid-der Box
Nail Board Design
Paper Bag Kickball
Pegboard Pictures
Pizza Pin-Ups
Playing Hooky
Poke & Peek
Quick & Easy Doll Clothes
Ring the Blade
Rings to String
Rolling Art
Scrambled Stickers
Shoe Box Train
Simple Sorting
Soap Bottle Pull Toy
Soda Pop Drop
Take Apart People
Take Apart Teddy
Target Toss
Top the Box
Tray Tie-Ups
Twist & Turn
Ziploc Dot-to-Dot

EQUIPMENT

Child Safe Bulletin Board
Child Size Game Net
Easy Flannel Board
Ice Cream Bucket Chair
Instant Paintbrush
Paper Bag Kickball
Puppet Stand
Ring Around the Baby
Scissors Holder
Simple Puzzle Repair